HAY HOUSE BASICS

THE
AKASHIC
RECORDS

THE
AKASHIC
RECORDS

Unlock the Infinite Power, Wisdom and Energy of the Universe

SANDRA ANNE TAYLOR

HAY HOUSE

Carlsbad, California • New York City • London
Sydney • Johannesburg • Vancouver • New Delhi

Published and distributed in Australia by:
Hay House Australia Ltd, 18/36 Ralph St, Alexandria NSW 2015
Tel: (61) 2 9669 4299; Fax: (61) 2 9669 4144; www.hayhouse.com.au

First published and distributed in the United Kingdom by:
Hay House UK Ltd, Astley House, 33 Notting Hill Gate, London W11 3JQ
Tel: +44 (0)20 3675 2450; Fax: +44 (0)20 3675 2451; www.hayhouse.co.uk

Published and distributed in the United States of America by:
Hay House Inc., PO Box 5100, Carlsbad, CA 92018-5100
Tel: (1) 760 431 7695 or (800) 654 5126; Fax: (1) 760 431 6948 or (800) 650 5115
www.hayhouse.com

Published and distributed in the Republic of South Africa by:
Hay House SA (Pty) Ltd, PO Box 990, Witkoppen 2068
info@hayhouse.co.za; www.hayhouse.co.za

Published and distributed in India by:
Hay House Publishers India, Muskaan Complex, Plot No.3, B-2,
Vasant Kunj, New Delhi 110 070
Tel: (91) 11 4176 1620; Fax: (91) 11 4176 1630; www.hayhouse.co.in

Distributed in Canada by:
Raincoast Books, 2440 Viking Way, Richmond, B.C. V6V 1N2
Tel: (1) 604 448 7100; Fax: (1) 604 270 7161; www.raincoast.com

A catalogue record for this book is available from the British Library.

ISBN: 978-1-78180-711-8

This book is dedicated to my parents,
Ronald and Sarah Marie Klingler
who are still guiding me from the
beautiful Akashic Realm.

Contents

List of Exercises

Acknowledgments

With deep love and appreciation to my family – Benjamin Earl Taylor Jr., Sharon Klingler, Vica Taylor and Ethan Taylor, Jenyaa Taylor and Ashley Taylor, Devin Staurbringer, Yvonne Taylor, and Kevin and Kathryn Klingler.

Deep appreciation to the incredible people at Hay House UK, including Michelle Pilley, Amy Kiberd, Sandy Draper, and Rachel Dodson; and unending gratitude to my Hay House family in the U.S., including Louise Hay, Reid Tracy, Margarete Nielsen, Christy Salinas, Shannon Godwin, Anna Almanza, Richelle Zizian, Laurel Weber, Mollie Langer, Christa Gabler, Tricia Breidenthal, Wioleta Giramek, Shay Lawry, Nicolette Young, Erin Dupree, and *all* of the other lovely men and women at this wonderful publishing company. And so very much appreciation to the phenomenal team at HayHouseRadio.com®, including Diane Ray, Rachel Fernandes, Kyle Thompson, Mitch Wilson, and Rocky George III. You're the best!

For their tireless effort and support, Rhonda Lamvermeyer, Marilyn Verbus, Andrea Loushine, and Cheri Polk. Thank you!

So much appreciation to my inspiring colleagues: Greg Braden, John Holland, Bruce Lipton, Darren Weissman, Denise Linn, Lisa Williams, Donna Eden, David Feinstein, Peggy Rometo, and Colette Baron-Reid.

To the family of my heart – Marilyn Verbus; Barbara Van Rensselaer; Ed Conghanor; Linda Smigel; Julianne Stein; Carmine and Marie Romano; Melissa Matousek; Tom and Ellie Cratsley; Karen and Dennis Petcak; Valerie Darville; Esther Jalylatie; and Dolores, Donna, Kathy, Tara and Adam Maroon – so much love to you all.

To my spirit family – Sarah Marie Klingler, Ron Klingler, Anna and Charles Salvaggio, Rudy Staurbringer, Candace Pert, Michele Jacobs, Earl Taylor, Chris Cary, Pat Davidson, Flo Bolton, Flo Becker, Tony, Raphael, Jude, and all the others who open the Akashic Records to me every day. And of course the Divine Consciousness that lives in all things and loves in all ways.

Finally, I want to thank *you* so very much – all of you who have shared your beautiful energy and support in so many ways and have brought so very much value to my life! It is my wish that the ideas and techniques in this book bring you the kind of happiness and empowerment they have brought my clients and me. May your life be blessed with increasing enlightenment and unceasing joy!

Introduction

Many books have been written about the Akashic Records. The approach to this life-changing source of information is as vast and varied as the number of philosophies and spiritual practices throughout time and across the world.

The Akashic Records are a vibrating storehouse of information and energy, an ever-present resonance that expands in our lives and in the Universe itself. They are in the smallest particle and the greatest field. They *are* the particle, the wave, the consciousness, the energy, and the information of eternity. Embodying all the mysteries of life – your life, my life, the entirety of life from before life began, as we know it – the records will go on long after the world that we know disappears.

This makes the Akashic Records sound very mysterious, but it is my intention to demystify them. Although they are esoteric, they are also very practical, and can be applied to any endeavor in our lives.

Most people use the Akashic Records to find out how the events from the past are influencing them now – whether from this or previous lives. While this isn't by any means the only purpose of investigating the Akashic Records, it is a very compelling one.

There is a longing that each of us has to change our difficult circumstances, to understand how and why things happen as they do, and to heal and empower ourselves in ways that will make our lives better and far happier. The information in the Akashic Records can help us to achieve all of these things, which is why the interest in this process is expanding so significantly. You have the power to look through the records of your eternal life and view the long-ago past, as well as the potential future. As you scan what happened to you in the past, you will see the patterns that are still influencing you today. You will be able to find previously unknown relationships with surprisingly familiar people. And you will recognize the sources of the problems, projects, issues, and goals that you are still dealing with today.

This is quite empowering because you are not only able to glean the information you need, you also have the ability to change your past records and shift present patterns in order to bring the resolutions that you're longing for.

Tapping into the power of the records

Connecting with the Akashic information and energy isn't difficult, for the records vibrate all around you – and even within you. They are held in the ethers and energies of the world, and they can be opened at any time you desire. They exist in each soul, in the cells of each body, and in the eternal mind. You can reach outward and inward, back in time – and forward too – to change your life in significant ways.

Some people say that you have to go through elaborate routines to open the records, but it's much easier than that. The exercises and techniques included in this book are all designed to help you open the Akashic Records and receive information in specific ways for specific purposes. In fact, as you work through these processes, you will find that you are living in a more receptive state to all of the types of information held in the Akashic Records. And you will be amazed at the many wonderful and even spontaneous ways that you can be inspired and informed.

You may also see as you go through this book that your intuition is being sparked more and more. Don't be surprised if you start connecting with spirit and feeling their remarkable presence in increasing areas of your life. After all, your work with the records not only brings past, present, and future potential, it also brings earthly knowledge and heavenly truth. It opens the energetic power of the spirit realm where you can forge lifelong connections with the angels, guides, and loving spirit who are always present and who long to assist you in any way they can.

The world of spirit freely travels in the Akashic Field, ready to connect with you, inspire you, and bring you guidance that can brighten your life. In fact, great discovery, art, expression, and creativity are all yours for the asking when you open the doors to the unlimited wisdom in the Akashic Realm!

Journeying into the Akashic Field, you can visit and rewrite your records of the past and get rid of difficult blocks in the present, heal relationship and financial patterns, and change the history of certain times and places that may still have a hold on you.

In addition to that, you can dramatically change the nature of your Present Records. By consciously recording your thoughts and actions now, you shift the very quality of your life. This improved energy dynamic then orchestrates new Future Records and a far better destiny.

And speaking of the future, you can go into the Akashic Records to do some future gazing. Since that dimension is vibrating in pure potential, the wisdom you bring back from that exercise can help you determine what needs to be done to create the results you want, and even program your Future Records with the achievements, emotions, and experiences you desire.

These are just some of the valuable reasons for reading and activating the Akashic Records. From understanding the workings of the Universe to working on your present relationships, from coming up with a new invention or a novel to coming up with a brand new future, the Akashic Records can bring wisdom, guidance, and energy to all of your intentions. And no matter what your intentions may be, it's always helpful to keep a Record Journal. After all, when you write about your written records, it clarifies and accelerates your processes of creation.

Your Record Journal

If you've read my other books you'll know that I always recommend keeping a journal, both to ventilate your ongoing feelings and to gain a deeper understanding of them. When working with the Akashic Records it's especially helpful because the simple process of writing about your experiences is an important piece of gaining clarity about your records.

First, I would recommend keeping a journal about some of your daily activities and emotions. When you read Chapter 7 and realize that you are writing your own records every single moment, keeping a journal of your life will help you to become conscious of your energy and its influence. Keeping a daily journal will also enlighten you as to which issues, projects, or concerns you want to prioritize in your Akashic Records excursions.

In addition, I recommend that you keep your journal near your bedside to record any information that may come in dreams, as these are a very powerful way to open the records and receive inspiration.

You can even focus your intention in your Record Journal before you fall asleep, requesting the kind of information you desire. If you are working on a creative project or a discovery of some kind, you can write that at the top of the page and request information on that. And if you are interested in some past-life information, you can write that at the top of the page and request information about that as well. Of course, your dreams don't always have to be directed. The answers that you need in your life often come unbidden, a result of your underlying intention and your desire to connect with record information and inspiration.

You can also use your Record Journal to jot down your impressions after doing the exercises in this book. Once you start following the processes, you will receive more intuitive messages, and you can jot those down as well. It's important to trust what your intuition tells you and let yourself experiment with the information you receive from the records themselves.

Don't become overwhelmed by all the suggested techniques. You don't have to do it all at once. It was my desire to offer a lot of options in these exercises so that you can use the ones that resonate with you most.

I have come to believe that pretty much everything is in the records, and we just have different forms of accessing that information. In fact, much of the research I have carried out over the years when writing my books (*see page 233*), has lead me to believe that information was stimulated either directly or indirectly through the Akashic Realm.

The quantum physics of the records

I have been writing and speaking about how the human experience is reflected in the principles of quantum physics for decades now. And I have seen over and over again how these principles clearly apply to our individual lives, as well as to the world at large. One important theory is the Heisenberg Uncertainty Principle, which indicates that the Universe exists in a state of flow or flux, where change can happen at any time. This potential for change – and the quality of our lives now and in the future – is the reason I have written this book. All of our outcomes exist in energetic potential and even the slightest change that we make now can create dramatically divergent results in our destiny. The ultimate solution is to reclaim our power, determining what we write in every present moment.

In fact, this has been the driving force behind all of my books, to encourage people to take charge of their lives and to use all of the tools at their disposal. Since the quantum physical principles of energy and consciousness underpin our resonant truth, and are also an important part of our Akashic Records, you will find these principles discussed in this book. If you want to look more deeply into the theories of consciousness creation and other parts of Universal Law, I recommend taking a look at my books, *Quantum Success, Secrets of Attraction*, and other previous books. If you want more detail on investigating and changing past-life influences, please check out *The Hidden Power of Your Past Lives*, which delves into that experience a little more deeply. It also has a free CD with past-life regression and rescripting, and though the processes in that book and CD are somewhat different than the past-life processes here, they can be helpful as well. I also want to mention that the karmic causes discussed in both of these books are sourced in the Edgar Cayce material, which I find to be the most compelling regarding these issues.

Whether you're interested in the past or the future, the Akashic Records can open the world for you. You can receive inspiration on any project you desire, enhance your present talents and find new ones, and use the records for prediction and decision-making. Whether finding new love or a new place to live, the Akashic records can assist you in your goal. You can also use Akashic Wisdom to connect with your purpose and find profound inner peace. By learning how to read the records, you will open yourself to a world of unlimited possibilities and a life filled with joy and discovery. Enjoy your journey. When you start using the Akashic Search Engine to find what you're looking for, life will never be the same again!

Part I

WHAT ARE THE AKASHIC RECORDS?

'There is a thinking stuff from which all things are made, and which in its original state, permeates, penetrates, and fills the interspaces of the Universe.'
W.D. Wattles

Chapter 1
Welcome to the Records

Wouldn't it be wonderful to have a library full of all the information you could ever need – about yourself, about the world, about what's going to happen 10 days from now, and what happened to you 200 years ago? Well, that library actually exists, and you can have access to it any time you like. That library is called the Akashic Records, and it is an unending source of information, inspiration, and energy that can totally change your life!

Interest in the Akashic Records has grown immensely in recent decades, especially for those who are seeking achievement, healing, and personal growth. In addition, the records are vastly appealing to those who long to be inspired. Whether it's for artistic or poetic expression or medical or scientific discovery, the Akashic Records can bring power, energy, and valuable information to anyone who desires to connect with this dynamic force.

What's in the records?
The term Akashic comes from the Sanskrit word *akasa*, which means sky or ethers. This represents the unending

expanse of vibrating consciousness that is both our shared and individual truth. Every energetic vibration of thought, emotion, and information – including your personal information from your own eternal history – is in the Akashic Records. Your past-life experiences, relationships, and conclusions – all that has led to your present identity – can be found there. In addition, the records can reveal your future potential, the vibrating possibilities waiting to be fulfilled or changed based on your present energy and direction.

In fact, the Akashic Records hold pretty much everything you would need to know about anything. They are alive with energetic vibration and endless information about the world and everything in it. On a personal level, they hold information from your eternal history, past, present, and future. And it may be an important part of your spiritual path to find out which past lives are still influencing this life, and what you can do to change things.

Most people focus on their present experience as a jumping-off place for what they want to search for in the Akashic Records. You may look for healing solutions or perhaps inspiration for a new invention or creative career. You might also search the records for explanations about why present goals seem to keep getting blocked. For example, if you're working on resolving problems with health, relationships, or money, you might investigate the possible past-life influences on this life. Once you look into the Akashic Records, you can see the causal connections and make the changes you are longing for in the present. In fact, personal healing – no matter what the issue – can be one of the most dynamic purposes for this pursuit.

But the Akashic Records go beyond the personal experience. They also include *all* the information concerning the entirety of the human and soul experience, including physical truth and undiscovered knowledge. All of the wisdom of existence, biology, science, quantum physics, and all the principals of natural law – both known and unknown at the present time – are vibrating in the Akashic Field, as well as all the wisdom of spiritual existence.

The records contain information that is both fixed and evolving. The fixed information is largely made up of spiritual truth. Almost everything else evolves and changes. In fact, the world, and all life in it, always exists in a state of vibrational potential, and as change occurs, the information in the Akashic Records changes as well.

The Akashic Records can be defined as a vibrating field of information about the energetic and natural worlds, about your own soul and eternal existence, and about every soul consciousness throughout time. The records span eternity and hold every bit of Universal information – from the wisdom of ancient societies to the discoveries yet to be made in the quantum physical world.

The history of the Akashic Records

Many cultures, religions, and philosophies throughout time refer to the records of life, although they have not always been called the Akashic Records. Mystical, yet comprehensive, the records are referred to in many ancient societies, including the Assyrians, Phoenicians, and Babylonians.

The Old Testament refers to the 'Book of the Living,' and the New Testament has several references to the 'Book of Life,' the unlimited information that will be opened in what is called 'the last days.' This is also said to include the records about who is admitted to heaven.

The angel Metatron is considered to be one of the oldest angels of the Hebraic tradition. He was called the scribe or the recording angel, and was said to have written down every action of every individual. In the Babylonian *Talmud* he was said to teach schoolchildren, and in later mystical texts he was said to guide people through heaven and explain its wonders.

In spite of these and many other references in the ancient world, the actual term 'Akashic Records' seems to date back to the mid- to late 1800s. The first published reference to the records of the *Akasha* appears in the late 1800s by H.P. Blavatsky (1831–91), the founder of the Theosophical Society, who said:

> Akasha *is one of the cosmic principles and is a plastic matter, creative in its physical nature, immutable in its higher principles. It is the quintessence of all possible forms of energy, material, psychic, or spiritual; and contains within itself the germs of universal creation, which sprout forth under the impulse of the Divine Spirit.*

Rudolph Steiner, who was born in Austria in 1861, was another proponent of the power and purpose of the Akashic Records. He believed that people could see past their physical senses to perceive deeper reality and truths unavailable to the naked eye. About this process he said:

A man broadens his power of cognition in this way if he is no longer limited to external evidence where knowledge of the past is concerned. Then he can see in events what is not perceptible to the senses... It is a fact that this history is written in other characters than is ordinary history... it is called the Akasha Chronicle.

Similarly Alfred Percy Sinnett, who wrote *Esoteric Buddhism* in 1884, defined the Akashic Records as a permanency of records in the *akasa* (or the ethers, *see page 3*). He said that anyone had the ability to read this information in the etheric realm through the intuitive mind. Other contemporaries who have taught these principles include Alice Bailey, Charles Leadbeater, Max Heindel, and Edgar Cayce, among many others.

Edgar Cayce and the Akashic Records

The modern mystic Edgar Cayce wrote extensively about the Akashic Records. Born in 1877, Cayce lived a relatively ordinary life in his youth, but around the turn of the century, he found that he had profound intuitive abilities. In a process that today would be called the work of a medical intuitive, Cayce would relax and achieve some kind of altered state, proceeding to dictate answers to people's medical questions, giving healing suggestions that would offer cures – or at least relief.

He conducted thousands of these sessions, which he called 'readings.' Each one was meticulously recorded and numbered by a stenographer, and the subject matter ranged from anything regarding an individual's health to very spiritual matters and questions about the past, the future, and other realms and plains of existence.

When asked where he got the information he received in his readings, Edgar Cayce replied that it was either from the individual's subconscious mind or the Akashic Records. In one of his readings he describes both the expansiveness and the individuality of the experience:

> *The entity itself sees, and is being taught... the records that are written in nature, in the rocks, in the hills, in the trees, in that termed the genealogical log of nature itself. Just as true, then, is the record that the mind makes upon the film of time and space in the activities of a body with its soul...*
> EDGAR CAYCE, READING 487-17

This quote reveals three important truths:

1. The records exist all around us.

2. We can see and be taught by them.

3. We ourselves are recording information through the activities of our own mind, body, and soul.

Although many people believe the Akashic Records have no physical manifestation, Edgar Cayce believed that in addition to being a vibrating field of information existing in all nature, they have a physical manifestation here on Earth. In fact, he believed that when we were ready to understand them, they would be found in one of three places – in the Yucatan, off the coast of Bimini, or buried in the Egyptian sands beneath the Great Sphinx.

Cayce only accepted donations for his readings, yet often received nothing, due to his belief that it was his personal responsibility to society – and to the individuals who wrote to him – to work in this capacity of service. Once, while doing a reading for a supplicant, he received information for himself. He was told that he was essentially working too much, and if he did not slow down and reduce the number of readings he gave each day, it would affect his health.

Cayce felt compelled, however, by the unending stream of letters he received from hopeful people all over the world who felt that he could help them, as he had helped so many others. He was driven by compassion, and he did not slow down. As his reading foretold, he did get sick, and he passed away within the year.

This demonstrates one of the many valuable purposes of the Akashic Records, witnessing a future potential and being given the opportunity to change it. In fact, I have seen several cases of those who have used the records for learning potential futures – and for recording the Future Records they desired.

Getting the job

While doing a record viewing of a potential future event, one woman witnessed herself in a disastrous job interview. As a result, she prepared her presentation in a different way and even wore different clothes. She visualized a different experience and a better outcome and then she placed that vision in her Future Records. Her resulting interview was completely changed, and she got the job.

A modern view

From the Tibetan view of the etheric realm to present philosophical and psychological concepts – and even to modern science, there is logic behind this theory of an all-encompassing information field. Two modern terms that refer to the expansiveness of this phenomenon are the 'Universal Mind' and the 'Cosmic Consciousness.' These refer to the shared consciousness of all humans – and even all spirit – relating to their existence individually and together. The fact is we share consciousness through our connection with each other, through our energy, and through the history and environment that we all share. The Akashic Records represent all of that, and they expand with every moment of our personal and shared contributions.

In his book, *The Turning Point*, the Austrian-born American physicist Fritjof Capra talks about the 'collective unconscious,' a shared consciousness that is embedded in everything and everyone. This represents the profound nature of the Akashic Records; they are timeless, comprehensive, and accessible. The fact that each and every one of us is a part of the records – and that they are a part of us – makes it eminently possible to open our minds and hearts to the information and energy stored there.

The Alaya Consciousness

Long before the term Akashic Records became popular, the Buddhist concept of the 'Alaya Consciousness' was being studied and embraced. This is actually my favorite name for this timeless concept because it embodies the two most important qualities that the Akashic Records represent. One truth can be found in the first word of this all-encompassing name, *alaya*, the Sanskrit term for 'unending' or 'without limit.' In fact, the name *Himalayas* is Sanskrit for 'unending snows.'

Alaya Consciousness, therefore, means unending information or limitless consciousness. The word 'consciousness,' gives the concept the living, vibrating quality that is so important in understanding the truth of the Akashic Records.

But what exactly does consciousness mean?

Scientists often define consciousness as a vibrating field of information, not a stagnant, unchanging list of facts, but a vibrant, expanding field of information. This field of information already exists and yet consistently vibrates in change and future potential. As we investigate it, we change it. It expands with energy, information, and influence – not only for us but for everyone.

The Alaya Consciousness is *about* everything in the Universe – and it's *within* everything in the Universe. It's in the subtle energies of each individual and in Divine Consciousness as well. Each of us has an eternal identity, a spiritual self that lives forever. Our eternal consciousness grows and evolves, as it experiences different things. As time goes on, it encodes different information and emotions from past lives and from present experiences and relationships. And every bit of it gets recorded in the Akashic Field.

> *Working with the Akashic Records, we realize*
> *the depth and distance of our connections.*

Our consciousness is always interacting, vibrating in resonance with others far and wide. Quantum physics has shown that influence happens at a distance. Information, communication, even precognition connects us with those we love, and amazingly, with those we don't even know.

As we shall see, those connections can lead to great discovery and creativity, and you too can use the information in the Akashic Records to inspire you in everything from your personal goals to your moneymaking activities. I've seen this with countless people in their personal and professional endeavors.

Paul's famous dreams and record inspirations

Paul McCartney woke up one day after dreaming about a song. The melody was so familiar to him that he was sure someone else had written it, and he was just remembering it. After lots of research he realized that wasn't the case, so he wrote it himself. That song was 'Yesterday,' and it became one of the most covered songs in musical history.

There was also a time when Paul was troubled about something and he had a dream in which his mother, whose name was Mary, came to give him advice. The song (and the advice) that came out of that dream was 'Let It Be,' a song that has been an inspiration to millions of people, including me.

This may be spectacular, but it's not unusual. One man I know used a record inspiration to come up with a computer app that brought his company millions of dollars. Another woman went into her record connections to find a buyer for her house.

But the greatest connection of all is our union with Divine Consciousness. The information held in the energetic or etheric realm reveals our powerful connection to a higher consciousness. Whether you believe this is a single entity or what is called the Oversoul of all life, it is certainly creative, loving, and powerfully healing. From the first thought in prehistory to every cell in the present Universe, life is expressing itself in endlessly changing connections. All of life reflects and projects Divine energy and vibration. The beauty of this is the unlimited potential of change. As we shift our consciousness to our true power, we can change our experience in this Universe, and we can even change the Universe itself.

This is another important purpose of the Akashic Records, to investigate past influences in order to alter present energy and future events. This vast storehouse of information can assist us in every area of our lives. When we begin to tap into the revelations that are waiting there, we find that we have the power and resources to heal physical problems, resolve relationship issues, and even change difficult financial patterns. All we have to do is connect with this wonderful source and get ready to receive!

Getting ready to receive

There are many things that you can do to prepare yourself to access the Akashic Records. As we shall soon see, the process does not have to be laborious or complicated. Although many people think that you have to follow very rigid steps and even use specific – and sometimes ancient or foreign – invocations to gain access to the records, it is a far easier process than that. And there are certain things that you can do in your everyday life to get ready.

Here are some simple activities you can engage in to become more receptive and make the Akashic Records more readily available to you:

♦ **Open your mind to the truth, guidance, and help that the Akashic Records can bring you.** As we shall see, there is much assistance available within this never-ending compendium of information. It can be used to help you in your personal, professional or romantic life. It can also bring amazing inspiration, creativity, and discovery that you may never have thought possible. So let yourself embrace the belief in this powerful tool. Use the exercises in this book and open your mind to the infinite possibilities.

♦ **Meditate as much as possible.** If you can meditate at least a little bit each day, you will achieve a level of consciousness that is far more open to receiving. Some people may find it difficult or feel too busy to meditate. If you are one of them, start with just a few minutes a day. Take a few minutes to breathe deeply, turn off your mind, and relax. It doesn't matter what form of meditation you use, as long as you allow yourself to mentally let go and relax. (*See below for a suggested meditation.*)

♦ **Do some deep breathing every hour or two.** The process of deep breathing can help bring both physical and mental relaxation, which is a good foundation for any Akashic exploration. It's also a great way to increase the harmony in your life and the clarity in your thoughts. So remember to take one or two deep breaths to clear your mind, center your energy, and bring peace to your present intention.

✦ **Affirm that you are open, capable, and deserving of receiving.** It's important that you see this exploration as something that is not only your right, but is also within your reach. This information is not limited to a few 'special' people. You *are* special. You have the light of the Divine within you, and you are worthy of using and enjoying this valuable tool.

✦ **Get out of your head and live in your heart.** The amount of time and energy we spend in our heads, brooding and worrying, can shift our energy and make it much more difficult to receive the guidance that we need. As much as possible, let go of the analysis, judgment, and worry, and let yourself relax in the peace of your heart. The meditation exercise below can help you do just that. Use it often – even if just for a few moments at a time.

These are just a few of the simple things you can do every day to balance your energy and get prepared for the incredible changes that await you once you start your journey into the Akashic Field.

Exercise: Heart-centered meditation

The following exercise can help you to quiet your mind and open your heart center, making you much more receptive to the information and power held in the etheric realm, the vibrating consciousness of the Akashic Field.

If you're not accustomed to meditating, just let your muscles relax and your mind quieten down. You don't have to strive or try to achieve some unusual state of mind. In fact, it's best to let go of analysis completely. Simply breathe deeply and be in the moment.

Gently follow the steps below. Trust in your process and in time you'll be meditating with comfort and ease.

1. Take a deep breath and notice what's on your mind. Just consider it and see where your thoughts lead and how they make you feel.

2. Take another deep breath and with your eyes closed, visualize those thoughts lifting out of your head and drifting away like a cloud. Just let them go far off into the distance, until they totally disappear.

3. Taking one more deep breath let the muscles in your head and shoulders relax.

4. As you relax even further, let your consciousness slowly drift down into your heart center.

5. With each easy breath, your conscious gently floats into your heart center where peace and tranquility abide.

6. And as your consciousness rests in that beautiful, peaceful place, you sense the spark of Divine Love that is vibrating deep within you.

7. Feel the peace and light of your own eternal heart filling you up, bringing a wonderfully tranquil yet radiant vibration to every part of you.

8. Feel the sense of familiarity and comfort that comes from being here, in your heart center.

9. Here you are peaceful and calm, yet deeply connected to your own eternal spirit, open to receiving guidance and inspiration at any time.

10. Continue to let yourself relax in this place and live in this peace as often as possible. This is your eternal source.

The Akashic Forces

This peace of the heart is one of the grand Akashic Forces, one of the eternal qualities that you can tap into at any time. The Akashic Forces are the valiant energies of the soul, the higher qualities that humans have aspired to achieve throughout the ages. They exist in the records of history and thought, and they vibrate through time, sending love, courage, wisdom, integrity, grace, compassion, industry, creativity, and so much more.

Just as your eternal information is available through the Akashic Records, so too are these qualities. They live in the human spirit, though they are often lost in distraction and disbelief. Yet the records of each soul hold the memory and truth of these wonderful powers deep within the heart, the center of the soul. The holographic meditation in Chapter 9 (*see page 179*) can help you experience these profound energies, or you can call upon them by name and meditate on their presence in your heart.

The forces of courage and love

I once had a client who was severely alcoholic. In a past-life viewing (see page 104) he saw that his wife and children were with him in a previous alcoholic life, one in which he was physically brutal. He was ashamed of his behavior then, and very remorseful. He did rewrite that Past-life Record (see page 110) but he really wanted to focus on what he was writing today.

So he also used the Present-record technique (see page 139), and every time he longed for a drink, he stopped and saw the image of that choice cast in his Present and Eternal Records. It made him sick to think about the repeated betrayal of his family and the weakness within himself. So he centered his consciousness in his heart and called upon the Akashic Forces of courage and determination. He used the force of love for his family to conquer his addiction, and over time he and his family left that experience behind and shifted their shared records forever.

The more you learn to live in your heart center, the more receptive you will be to receiving life-changing energy and information from the Akashic Records. Your connections to others – and to the solutions you seek – are held there in ready availability. Open your heart to the inspiration that's waiting to take your life in wonderful new directions.

SUMMARY

- ✦ The Akashic Records date back to the Old Testament and early Buddhist writings but were written about extensively in the 19th century by Rudolph Steiner, H.P. Blavatsky, and Edgar Cayce.

- ✦ Three important truths revealed by the records are that they exist all around us, we can see and be taught by them, and we are recording information all the time.

- ✦ Practices that can help you tune in to the Akashic Records are meditation, deep breathing, and affirmations.

- ✦ Record guidance increases when you keep an open mind and focus on living out of your heart rather than the mind.

- ✦ The Akashic Forces are the valiant energies of the soul, and they vibrate through time, energy, and space throughout all the ages – past, present, and future.

Chapter 2
Energy and Information: Eternity Vibrating

It is well known how DNA can reveal amazing amounts of information about an individual. In a single cell, we can find out about a person's identity, lineage, potential for diseases, and much, much more. This is the Personal Record of one's physiology, representing each individual's biological nature.

Yet there is a storehouse of information that transcends even that staggering data of our DNA. It's about our history, our psyche, our energy, and even about our potential future. For each individual, each group, each culture and country, for the globe itself and far beyond, every bit of essence and experience is recorded in the Akashic Records, which, like our DNA, can first be found by searching within.

But the place and purpose of the records are unlimited in scope. The Akashic Records exist in time, space, consciousness, and energy. From the petal of a flower to the beat of your heart, from a distant star to a tiny pebble under your foot, the records are within and all around you. Eternity and infinity are mapped in your records. They can be accessed whenever you desire and used for countless reasons, including investigating your past lives.

Karma, reincarnation, and your soul's map

Some people call the Akashic Records your soul's map. This is an apt description, for it can reveal where you've been, where you are now, and where you're going. Each soul has its own path to follow, its own lessons from the past and its own unique goals for the future. You may get lost in your present pursuits, but you can always look at the records of your past lives – and your future intentions – to figure out what it is you need to do next. After all, this is not your first time around!

A simple interpretation of *reincarnation* states that the individual soul is born into a series of lifetimes and physical bodies, existing in an energetic – or some believe heavenly – realm between each incarnation. Within this system of repeated lifetimes, karma is formed. Karma is very often defined as the workings of the Law of Cause and Effect, but it's really the vibrations of our accumulated choices, conclusions, and emotions that become a part of our Personal Records.

This data is also encoded in our eternal consciousness where our experiences of behavior, thought, and feeling build a repeated resonant momentum. These patterns repeat in our energy, projecting our most predominant vibrations, attracting experiences that either challenge us or bring us joy. In that way our karma, or energetic history, then goes on to direct our personal destiny in the present and in future lifetimes. But it is this present life that gives us the power to make all the desired changes in our energetic makeup, a process that makes the study of reincarnation truly valuable.

As I described in the previous chapter, Edgar Cayce used the Akashic Records to do nearly 2,000 readings of past lives but he also used them to find out important diagnostic and healing information for his clients – and to look into the future to make many predictions (*see page 7*).

You can follow all of these pursuits when investigating the records for yourself. Finding out about your past-life events and relationships can be a fascinating adventure. Yet it's the process of applying that information to healing present problems that really brings the Akashic Records to life.

Valuable record reasons

There is so much power and potential waiting in the records. When you learn how to explore this valuable source of energy and information, you will be able to:

✦ Find out how past lives have influenced your present relationships, including romantic, parental, friendship, and work relationships.

✦ Learn past-life sources of present problems and patterns, including fears, depression, shyness, addictions, and even such things as chronic poverty and loneliness.

✦ Get specific information on how to heal and reverse these unwanted physical, emotional, financial, and relationship patterns.

- ✦ Find your personal purpose and live a more conscious and fulfilling life.

- ✦ Learn about global energies and issues, including social, cultural, religious, and military patterns – past, present, and future.

- ✦ Expand your intuition and receive powerful intuitive messages on a regular basis.

- ✦ Receive data and inspiration regarding any project, whether medical, technical, financial, scientific, or any other pursuit.

- ✦ Find and enhance your natural talents, whether musical, artistic, athletic, or any other activity.

- ✦ Receive assistance in making important decisions.

- ✦ Look into potential Future Records to determine what you can do now to change or enhance things in the time to come.

- ✦ Program events and outcomes into your Future Records for desired manifestation.

- ✦ Understand profound spiritual truths, learn how to expand your spiritual awareness, awaken to your Soul's Point of View, and establish a truly peaceful approach to life.

All of these activities and many more will not only help you to understand the meaning of your life, but they can also help to change both your energy and your future. But your focus on the Akashic Records is not limited to working on and for yourself. Your effort can garner important results for the friends, family, community, and even for the greater communities that inhabit this planet. In fact, the planet, along with everything on it, not only stores the information of the records and influences that information, but it also is very much influenced by the work you do in your record exploration. It is all a process of give and take, expansion of energy, and accumulation of information. And it's always as close as your own breath.

The hologram of life

The Akashic Records are not held within some mystical, etheric library located out in the stratosphere. They are vibrating histories, truths, and future potentials held in even the smallest places and timeless spaces. Every little thing in the Universe, every vibration and particle holds the records in their entirety. It's holographic in nature, and it's liberating to realize that this important information is available to us through so many sources.

The hologram has become a common phenomenon in everyday life, three-dimensional images seen in amusement parks, on TV, and in movies. Two laser beams creating an interference pattern on film produce the hologram picture. To produce the image, another laser light is shot through the film, which on the surface looks merely like a mass of shimmering, waving lines. But the image is held within the hologram – in fact, it's within every minute part of the hologram. If the film were to break into a dozen pieces, you could shine the light through the smallest piece and still see the complete image in its entirety.

The Akashic Records are holographic in nature.
Their truths are revealed in their entirety in every
piece of nature, every particle of sand, every
blade of glass and every wave on the shore, as
well as in every unseen and unheard vibration
around you. They are eminently accessible, always
resonating within you, waiting to be tapped.

Inner spaces

We know that the massive amounts of information in your DNA can be seen in each and every cell, but your body holds more information than that. Through the process called *cellular memory*, you hold countless records about yourself and your history – both in this life and in long-ago existences.

You may wonder how your physical cells can hold codes from previous lifetimes, but you might also be very surprised to find out that they hold the essence of stars that have existed for thousands of years.

Carl Sagan once said that we are all made of 'star stuff.' This is not just a poetic metaphor, it's an energetic and elemental truth, for the elements that were first formed in stars long ago are the same elements that allow us to live, function, and thrive today. It took those ancient suns millions of years to create the very atoms that make up every one of us. It is an elegant truth that we hold the history of all life within.

So it's clear that your cells, as a part of this amazing Universe, have already done a lot of work – and continue to hold untold records. But the greatest part of what is recorded within you is actually *about* you and your eternal life – past, present, and even potential future. These records are a part of your energetic body, the essence of your eternal light and vibration that reshapes itself in every new lifetime.

This energetic body, also called your etheric or astral body, is an important part of your Personal Records. Although this is an energy form, it vibrates with the records of your previous physical, emotional, and cognitive experiences. As you move through time, the events of the past – whether joyous or traumatic – are written in your records and in your energetic body – along with the emotions and beliefs that those events created.

In this way, the groundwork for new experiences in upcoming lifetimes is developed, and our predominant patterns are formed. The more emotionally charged the experience, the more influential that record becomes – until we take some action to change it. This is one reason why working with the Akashic Records can be so liberating. Once we find out what has happened, we can write a new record – one that empowers us and brings us a greater sense of our eternal value and worthiness, and one that changes what we're going through now.

Janet's freedom

I once had a client named Janet who had been physically abused in childhood. She walked with a slouch and was fearful of the world. She also had back problems, and the memories of past brutality had been stored in her cells there. We worked together on erasing the negative records of her past and writing new records

*of strength and safety. She also worked on creating
a clear and self-empowered Present Record, as well
as a Future Record of freedom and self-actualization.
Watching her transformation was a revelation to me.
She became a strong, self-assured woman and recorded
that for all time!*

You, too, can clear difficult records from your past – whether in this life or in previous ones. You don't have to be a mystic or a seer to find out what happened in your unknown past, or to learn how to deal with it now. The information exists within your Akashic energy, vibrating with amazing revelations and endless potential for change. With a little investigation, you can open up this eternal toolbox of change and enlightenment. It's not difficult to engage in this process, for the evidence of what you may need – or want – to work on is all around you, throughout your life, and in time itself.

Vortex of time

The records may be located in space and energy, but that's not all. It's easy to see how both good and bad memories can be held in a certain place. In fact, the places of our past can hold uncomfortable records and evoke unwanted memories and emotions. The energy lingers in the place and vibrates with information and feelings. And if repeated trauma was involved, that place could hold strong records of fear, anger, or resentment. You may never have to return to this place again, but if such a location exists for you, it would be helpful to do the 'Clearing the records of time and space' exercise later in this chapter (*see page 32*).

In addition to space, time itself can hold information as well. Each season is filled with very specific patterns of both energy and information. The stroke of midnight can carry important records, especially on certain days. A multitude of cultures and religions have poured powerful energy into the Akashic Records around their ceremonies and holidays.

December 25 and January 1 are just two of countless dates in the calendar that resonate with the energy of a shared vortex of time. However, the information around these two particular dates has been accumulating for centuries and continues to shift and change as the years progress. Even the date of September 11 now carries a powerful vortex of emotion. For many people, just seeing or saying the number 9/11 evokes highly charged images that are still held and repeated, swirling vibrations of fear, anger, and even hatred around that date.

Individual and group intentions are also recorded in certain times of the year. For example, the coming of fall (autumn) awakens plans of going to school, harvesting the land, and feasting. These and similar records are stored in countless time vortices into which we pour our shared experiences and emotional reactions. From the time of day, like the rising of the sun, to the time of year, like the falling leaves, there are subtle – and not so subtle – records that stimulate both shared memories and resonant intentions for many of us.

Your personal circles of time

It's important to know that each of us individually has Personal Records stored in time as well. In fact, you may be able to look at your life and recognize those times when certain patterns were repeated, revealing outright what your Personal Records may hold. And if you see a specific trend around certain dates or times – or patterns that are consistent to a specific time of the year – you can bet you've experienced those patterns at the same time in past lives.

For example, the last week of July is an important vortex of time for me – at least as I witness the patterns in this life. Three major relationships in my life, including my present marriage, were heralded in at that time. This is clearly a record of romantic experience, and I would wager that I have experienced the same type of events – perhaps even with the same people – at the same time in past lives.

Ted's circles of time

A similar, yet energetically opposite, situation became apparent in the life of a client of mine named Ted. He was engaged to be married and felt strongly that he needed to wait until the winter to hold the wedding. His fiancée resisted that choice, however, and eventually convinced him to bring forward the date to June. It was to be a rather elegant affair, but in the months leading up to the event, they found that they were having increasing difficulties in the relationship. It got so bad that Ted told his fiancée that he needed to postpone the wedding. His fiancée left, however, and their dreams for a happy future together went with her.

When we explored his Past-life Records, we found that this had been a life of repetition for them, each leaving

*the other several times before, often at the same time.
But the vortex of that particular week in June didn't
just hold the Eternal Records of their relationship, it
also held information and energy of other difficult
events in Ted's present life.*

*In our conversation about the importance of this time,
Ted started to tell me about previous incidents that
happened during the very same week in this life. First,
he experienced the death of his father. Then in another
year at the same time, his apartment was ransacked
and robbed, causing him to move to another state.
A few years later he was mugged, severely beaten,
and left for dead. All of these events were extremely
traumatic and, along with the recent break-up, created
a highly energized vortex of unsettling experiences in
the records of his life, for all of them happened in the
very same week!*

*Once we gathered all the information, Ted and I
worked on clearing the records, as well as the energy
stuck in the vortex of that particular week in time. We
created some affirmations of release, reclaiming his
power and peace of mind at that time. He also did a
meditation where he visualized a calendar covered with
writing. This represented the old negative patterns and
experiences – which he then saw being erased.*

*He then visualized a clear, shining, empty space on
that week in the calendar and filled it with words
and images that were pleasant and empowering to
him. In this way he wrote new records of happiness,
safety, and strength associated with the vortex of that*

time. Also, as he approached that week in real time,
he planned happy experiences and continued to do
empowering exercises like the one below.

Even the time of day can carry a vortex of energy for you. I have dealt with many people suffering from insomnia who experienced some traumatic event in the middle of the night in a past life. They carried the memory with them, and whenever that time of day came around, it triggered fear, dread, and the need to be ever-watchful, ever-awake. Yet even those difficult patterns can be erased. The memories can be cleared and the present problem greatly relieved.

Not every time vortex in the records of your life is filled with negative information. You may be able to look at your life and see patterns of positive experiences occurring during certain days, months, or seasons. These records tend to repeat themselves as well, but since they're pleasant and reassuring, there's no need to shift those records in order to create new energetic patterns. But if you do have a time or space vortex that's recorded with difficult experiences, you can clear those negative records and create new, positive trends for the future.

Exercise: Clearing the records of time and space

Consider the times of your life. Is there a certain day, week, month, or season that repeatedly brings challenges to you? Even the time of day could be important. Write down the pattern and identify the time in your Record Journal.

1. What behaviors, thoughts, or emotions do you experience at these times? List the difficult ones that you would like to clear.

2. Now list the pleasant and empowering emotions and energies you want to replace them with.

3. Visualize a calendar or clock in front of you indicating the time period you have in mind. You may see writing or even images depicting the events you want to clear. Simply see yourself erasing those words or images and creating a clear, bright space on the calendar or clock.

4. Now visualize new words appearing there, words like: power, joy, relaxation, fulfillment, achievement, and happiness. Fill the calendar or clock with beautiful color and light, and even joyous, peaceful images of yourself experiencing that time in the way you desire.

5. Next, consider any places where you've had consistently difficult experiences in this life. In your Record Journal, describe the patterns you notice taking place and the emotions they evoke.

6. Think about how you want to approach this place differently. Write the new beliefs and attitudes that you would like to bring into this place. Include things like self-empowerment; self-valuing, and peace of mind.

7. When you meditate, visualize an image of the place you have in mind and see yourself erasing any dark shadows. Affirm: 'I am releasing any toxic attachment to this place. I am free and peaceful in its presence.'

8. Then visualize a beautiful light surrounding this place. You can see yourself in the image, happy and strong, perhaps even getting taller than the place itself. You feel more empowered than ever before regarding this location.

If you ever have a reason to be in this place again, remember your new visualization, filling yourself with light and power. Breathe deeply and affirm, 'I have a history, but I am not my history. I am powerful and peaceful everywhere I go.'

Outer places of shared records

As I described earlier, just as our individual bodies carry the records, so do the bodies of animals, plants, and inanimate objects, as well as bodies of water, earth, and the endless sky. Like cells holding personal vibrations, places can hold the whole of the records as well as their own signature information.

Places like Ground Zero and the Wailing Wall hold very specific data in cascading frequencies that include names, intentions, strong emotions, and history. Countries hold a variety of records – for good or not – each of which is distinguishable from the rest. Think about the different information held in places such as Ireland, Israel, Iceland, or Iran. Even just the names of these places can evoke vastly different thoughts and emotional responses.

Streets also hold the records of the place and of the people who've traveled them, often in a buzzing resonance that can almost be heard. From Bourbon Street to Broadway, Charing Cross to the Champs Élysées, across the world a signature resonance is recorded in the bricks and the buildings – and the spaces in between.

So what does this mean for us? The fact is, the records are within us and all around us, and we can have access to the information held right where we are. It's also important for us to know that we – as individuals and as groups – feed the records and influence the energy of the places we are in – and even the places that we simply think about. What are your thoughts about your home, your town, or the places you visit or even just read about? You are funneling energy there, which the records will take note of and send back in your direction.

In this way, the records expand, and the information accumulates, gathering an energetic momentum in one direction or another. This creates a phenomenon known as 'morphic resonance,' a profound element of the human experience – and an important function of the Akashic Records.

Harvesting the morphogenetic fields

Fields are often described as forces of information that somehow influence the matter they surround, just as the power of the gravitational and electromagnetic fields are clearly visible in the orbit of the earth around the sun and in a compass pointing north. But there's much more to the field phenomenon than that. You have a Personal Energy Field that influences your own experience but also extends across time and space, having significant consequences in the lives of others.

All humans – past, present, and future – and all existence share a consciousness that expands and connects. That connection is not just an ephemeral concept, it's a very real energetic force of cause and effect, one that is made even more real by the amazing phenomenon of morphogenetic fields – a term coined in the 1980s by scientist Rupert Sheldrake in his book *A New Science of Life*. This is a vastly interesting concept because it reveals the power and influence of our personal energy and of the Akashic Records themselves.

Morphogenetic fields are filled with energy and information fed not only by individuals, but also by groups. This creates a group consciousness, an energetic field that then influences others within the group. Through the process that Sheldrake calls 'morphic resonance,' the fields expand, build momentum, and affect the experiences of the world. Specific knowledge and behavioral habits accumulate, and that accumulated consciousness grows in vibration. When it achieves a critical magnitude, it moves into the awareness of everyone in the species.

One example is the expansion of the digital age. The use of smartphones, tablets, the Internet, and other satellite-guided connections has exploded worldwide. So much so, it's hard to believe that just a few decades ago most of this technology didn't even exist.

Other morphogenetic fields can be seen in such periods as the Renaissance when the world evolved from the dark ages into incredible, expanding accomplishments in painting, sculpture, science, and exploration. The Industrial Revolution is another example, as it completely altered the way much of the world made its living, turning most of the world from an agrarian to an industry-based society, bringing millions of people into cities across the world.

This process of morphic resonance is an ever-changing part of the records, moving our species in very specific energetic directions. It's a vibrational domino effect. Consciousness expands knowledge and knowledge expands consciousness, until in time the changes take on a life of their own.

It's important to know that we share records with others, including those in our personal relationships, families, communities, cultures, religions, and countries. What we need to remember is that we have both the power and the purpose of clearing negative, unhealthy, or unloving energy from our personal and shared records. As we let go of judgment and create higher intentions regarding our perceptions of ourselves and others, we feed the morphogenetic fields of love and compassion. Those healing energies expand and reach out to influence others, bringing greater peace to the world.

This is one way we can use the Akashic Records to benefit both ourselves and others. It's an important vehicle for understanding and expansion. We can investigate the past and see the patterns that drove the world in a negative direction. Then we can write new records – and feed new fields – with joy, tolerance, trust, and understanding.

But to do this, we must bring our examination and intentions into our present choices. We must choose loving treatment and talk – both to ourselves and others. In this way, we can shift the expansion of fear and hatred by changing the records of our own emotions. As more and more of us engage in expanding the consciousness and records of love, we can move our shared experience in healthier and happier directions, changing the future and creating a more joyous destiny for all.

SUMMARY

♦ The Akashic Records exist in time, space, consciousness, and energy, and can reveal your past and potential future lives: where you've been, where you are now, and where you're going.

- ◆ Each soul has its own path to follow, its own lessons from the past, and its own unique goals for the future.

- ◆ Karma is the ongoing energy of your accumulated choices, conclusions, and emotions, all of which become a part of your Personal Records.

- ◆ The information in your Personal Records is ever changing, and it gathers with similar energies to expand a morphic resonance and exert influence in the world.

- ◆ We share records with others, including those in our relationships, families, communities, cultures, religions, and countries.

- ◆ We have the power to clear negative, unhealthy, or unloving energy from both our personal and shared records.

Chapter 3
The Records – Now and Always

Although the Akashic Records hold unlimited information about literally everything, many people limit their record exploration to past-life investigation. In the East, reincarnation is widely adopted as the basis of many religions. People in the West may have lagged in accepting this theory of transmigration of the soul, but the trend has changed dramatically in recent years. And now a vast number of Westerners believe in the concept.

The fact is, the theory of reincarnation makes sense – both energetically and personally. When you feel familiar with a new place or person, it could be a quiet memory vibrating in the depth of your eternal consciousness. A current talent could easily represent a past-life skill. Irresistible attraction now could indicate previous passions. And problems from long ago could be the source of such present patterns as addictions and obsessions.

You are an eternal being and your Personal Records hold the details of every experience in every life you've ever lived. The time of your life is now and always. Instead of ending, your spirit transforms, returning lifetime after lifetime. Through your many experiences, you form habits and attachments. Relationships, personality patterns, and emotions all get written in the records of your eternal life. Throughout time your consciousness carries the records of the eternal you in accumulated codes that direct your present path. So it becomes immensely helpful to explore the records to more easily understand the issues you're dealing with now. The information you uncover can not only reveal important truths about what you're going through, but also empower you to rewrite the unhealthy or unhappy records and move in new directions from now on.

Science, energy, and eternity

Aristotle stated, 'The more you know, the more you know you don't know.' This concept holds true today. Dark matter and dark energy make up 95 percent of our Universe, yet our physical world is only 4.9 percent. Just think how much there is to learn about!

One interesting theory about this incredible Universe of ours is M theory, which some scientists call the mother of all theories. This could help to explain the nature and behavior of all matter and energy. M theory's concept of 11 home dimensions being the source of untold numbers of parallel universes opens up eternal potentials of reality. Past-life events and future-life potentials coexist in the storage of unlimited information on membranes of consciousness that are as close to you as the end of your eyelashes.

On these membranes there are entire universes, mysterious realms holding worlds of reality. In our experience, this could mean that what is clear, true, and predictable may be only part of the story. Unlimited potential events far beyond our consciousness may exist in the records and could connect with these alternate realities.

It is possible to get a glimpse of both our past and potential future events actually located on other membranes due to the very nature of time. A large part of our awareness spins in the orbit of our present incarnation. But we are able to spring to the path of another life, gather information from the records there and examine the relevance and importance in our current experiences. This exploration can make a big difference in the events and emotions of this life. In fact, the opportunity to unravel karmic influences can transform everything!

When we understand that energy can be transferred and matter can be transformed, the principles of reincarnation and the continuum of life become clear. This is true on a cosmic level, and it applies to our individual lives and identities as well.

Reincarnation can clarify many unanswered questions. For example, why do some people suffer more than others? Perhaps it's not as arbitrary as many think – perhaps our perception of hardship is simply a return of energy that gives us the freedom to understand unlearned experiences from previous lifetimes.

Reincarnation could also explain the many questions we have about the experiences in our present life, such as meeting a new acquaintance and having the impression that we've known this person before, or the sudden and easy appearance of a skill or talent that's actually an extension from a past life. Also, emotional events such as love at first sight, an overpowering attraction or repulsion to someone, phobias, allergies, weight issues, and even sexual preferences might be linked through reincarnation. All of these things may have existing explanations, but an eternal view may make even more sense and provide a more thorough understanding.

Investigating your Past-life Records uncovers powerful yet unknown attraction factors, revealing how and why you have attracted certain life-shaping events, and released negative ones, as well as revealing potentially positive influences.

When you start to travel the records of your own past existences, you will get glimpses of past personalities and emotions felt before. This new awareness will give you deeper insight into why certain patterns, events, and ongoing choices rule your life now. With this new clarity, knocking down the obstacles and finding the changes you long for will become far easier.

Seeing the truth

One client had significant vision problems and severe chronic allergies. She also worked in a job she hated. When we looked into her Past-life Records, we found a life where she was a slave in Ancient Rome, and her job was to clean other people's clothes, stirring them in boiling concoctions that steamed awful-smelling fumes into her face. She resented both the work and the fumes that burned her eyes and made her sneeze.

When she looked at the situation of her present life, she realized that she was carrying those memories in her cells – and in her feelings of servitude in her present job. She rewrote those old records, and she worked on reclaiming her power in her present situation.

In time she was able to leave that job and find one that resonated with her. She also rid herself of some of her physical problems, reducing her allergies to merely seasonal instead of year round. And although she still needed glasses, she no longer had the pain and dryness that had plagued her for so long. Her lesson had been from the past, but she reclaimed her power in the present and released herself from future suffering. Such is the nature of time. Our power in the present leads us in both directions.

The nature of time

Time is elusive. We label it by hours, days, and years to define and compartmentalize our existence. We hold on to it in our minds, using both our memory and our sense of anticipation. If the past and the future exist in parallel universes, then different experiences today could lead to many possible alternatives to come. And this is not limited to just the future. Believe it or not, these shifts in consciousness could provide us with different pasts and presents as well.

Many scientists today believe that all time exists simultaneously. The perception of moment-to-moment in sequential time is more of an experiential phenomenon. This concept is called the space-time continuum, and though it's difficult to absorb, it basically says that all time exists at the same time.

Yet how can all of time – past, present, and future – exist simultaneously? And if this is really what's happening, as we travel through the present moment, what could be occurring in the future – and the past – at this very same instant? The answers are mind-boggling but very important.

Space-time continuum could be a deep, wide space phenomenon where movement can occur in one direction and at the same time in opposite directions. It could also be a field of potentiality where all past, present, and future potentials are present on the same plane. These different fields of potentiality express themselves at different rates of vibration. In other words, the past, present and future are happening simultaneously but resonating at different vibratory rates.

This means that linear movement, the ever-present now, is happening at a much denser resonance. This dense resonance allows us to live in what we call 'real' time, with all the physical sensations that entails. Our past then falls away in a less dense vibration, while our future plane opens up in front of us, energetically taking shape even now.

Our experience of sequential time is that linear moment. We are always in the 'now' in terms of what we see and feel. All the while, the rest of time is vibrating as pure potential in our lives. Past, present, and future all happening simultaneously offers a significant tool in dealing with our recorded codes and patterns. This gives us the opportunity to rewrite the records of the past, to choose consciously what we record in the present, and move forward to script the record details of the future.

Following the future

We will be exploring how the past is still influencing the present, and the specific steps we can take to change both. Later we will also be looking at how we can actually visit the future and even direct our destiny there – both in this life and in lifetimes to come.

But if all time exists at once, the question of predestination comes into play. If the future is happening at this very moment, does that mean that the events in the future are already set and established? I believe the answer is *no*. The future exists in energetic potential, not in predestined fact. As we change our energy – both past and present – we record different outcomes for all the time to come.

> *Our soul creates lessons for us, but our major life events are not scripted in advance, and they can be changed.*

The well-known Heisenberg Uncertainty Principle gives us insight into this complex idea. According to the Uncertainty Principle, our world exists in a state of pure potential, a constant state of flow and flux, where change can happen at any moment. This applies to the waves and particles of our physical world, and it's also true for our eternal lives. The soul brings its lessons into our existence, and the events that occur are there to help facilitate our growth. When we learn these lessons, we have the option to change what we're experiencing in the present. That change can then shift the energetic potential of the future as well. In other words, though the future is already vibrating in energetic potential, we always have the power to change it.

A revelation of Titanic proportions

One of the great purposes of the Akashic Records is for you to open up to the wisdom they hold and use your intention, consciousness, and energy to set the records straight. We can do this by rewriting the records of the past, but we can also take a look at the records that vibrate in future potential – not only to gain knowledge of what that future holds, but also to gain a better understanding of what changes we need to make now in order to create the best future possible.

There is a little-known but true and fascinating story that exemplifies the readiness of Future Records as well as the potential for change. In 1898 a man named Morgan Robertson wrote a book about a huge cruise ship that went down in the North Atlantic shipping lanes. It hit an iceberg on its starboard side, and sank in a matter of hours but because there were too few lifeboats on board, over 1,200 people were lost at sea.

Fourteen years *before* the sinking of the *Titanic*, Robertson wrote a book that had over a dozen exact parallels to that historic event. Amazingly, his book was called, *Futility: Or the Wreck of the Titan*. Later he talked about having a dream that was so compelling, he had to write about it. Clearly, he was exposed to the potential records of the event yet to come, incorporating many of the details, including something akin to the ship's name in his narrative.

This incredible coincidence begs the question:

*Is the future predestined? Does it
already exist in unchangeable fact?*

If it's not predestined, why did Robertson see this? That particular future event already existed in potential and the energies were already in play. Still, there were plenty of contributing factors where the people involved could have changed their energy and their choices, and therefore changed the results of the event. Yet they did not.

The main engineer had wanted to place enough lifeboats for everyone, but the designer said it would look too ugly on the deck, so he overrode that decision. They had been warned about the icebergs several times that night, but the need for speed – and the desire for future profits – made everyone dismiss those warnings. The individuals involved were clearly set on a course driven by personal agenda, and the factors came together to create the disastrous event that actually did happen years after Robertson wrote his book.

If, however, the money-driven priorities had been changed to a higher consciousness, and if the people in charge had had a higher regard for human life, that event could have been entirely avoided. A potentially different outcome existed, but the energy remained the same, rolling forward in waves of mistaken priorities and dismissive attitudes. This reveals the bottom-line truth:

*Energy determines events, and when energy
changes, both the results and the records
can turn out to be very different.*

Setting future intentions

So what does this mean for you personally? It means you can investigate the Akashic Records to see where your present energy is likely to lead you. As you do, you can determine what energies you want to change in order to create the kind of outcomes you truly desire. In addition to viewing potential futures, you actually have the power to *write* the records of your future. In this way, you can program the results and experiences that you're working toward into the record of your eternal soul. In fact, as we shall see later in the book, there are a number of ways that you can set your intentions in motion within the records. You can then align your own present energy with those recorded plans, directing your destiny with clarity and purpose.

It may be surprising to some, but you can also use the Akashic Records for such things as finding a job, picking a stock investment, choosing a new place to live, or even finding new love. Where the Akashic Records are concerned, you are at the center of a vibrating vortex of energy, intention, and information, one of the most powerful forces in the world.

Opening the record doors

There are many ways to tap into this incredible force. In fact, the connection can often come without your bidding. The revelations usually happen when you're relaxed, open, and receptive. This is usually a function of being in the alpha level of brain frequency, which is the most receptive and creative state of mind.

When your brain frequency rests between seven and 14 cycles per second, you're at the alpha level. This is the frequency of meditation and dreaming. Above 14 cycles per second is the beta level of waking, active life. Below seven is deep sleep or sometimes a state of trance. And although the best level for connecting with this powerful vortex of information is in the alpha state, it's not always necessary. Let's look at all the ways you can open the record portal.

✦ **Meditation:** Any meditation should lead you to the alpha level, which can bring spontaneous connection with the records. However, if you use a specific process with the intention to access the Akashic Field, such as the many meditation processes throughout this book, you will get more focused results. Play with the different exercises here and create some of your own. You never know when or how inspiration is going to strike!

✦ **Spontaneous inspiration, intuition, and dreams:** Many flashes of connection to the Akashic Records come without expectation. They often have something to do with an issue you're dealing with or a project you're working on because that is the predominant focus in your life. Yet sometimes they have nothing to do with the current concerns. Instead, they represent random thoughts, inspirations, or guidance rising up from the depths of the Akashic Field. Dreaming and daydreaming can be a source of connection, too. In fact, information often comes up when you're falling asleep or just waking up. So always keep a notebook by your bed to write your dreams and impressions.

◆ **Spirit messages:** There is a wealth of information that can be transmitted from the records directly to you by the way of heavenly messengers. Spirit folk, friends and family, guides and angels abound, and they are all willing to inform and inspire you. More information on these incredible resources can be found in Chapter 8, but the meditation process below will introduce you to one of your record guides. Be open to this experience, for it's the start of a wonderful journey.

◆ **Akashic Readings:** Many psychics, mediums, and intuitives delve into the Akashic Records to give readings of all sorts, including past-life readings. Perhaps because they open the door to the energetic realm so frequently, their access to the Akashic Records is more free flowing. When connecting with a client, they can pick up the resonance of that person's unique signature vibration, creating an automatic link to that person's particular life-force energy, receiving everything from guidance on present projects to past-life information that is still an influence today. You can even learn to give record readings yourself. When you open the pipeline to this wonderful energy, you'll be amazed at what you see.

Viewing the records

People see the Akashic Records in many different forms. Some people perceive them as a book, a large old volume that, when asked a question, has the ability to open to the right page to provide the answer. Many others see the records as a library with countless books and scrolls.

Far fewer people see the records as playing out on a screen, a sort of digital version for modern times. Coming up later in this book you'll find exercises using many of these forms, and since the information is vibrating all around you, you can view the records in any way that is comfortable for you. Even if you choose to see the records in a large book, don't be surprised if detailed images appear and actually start to move on the page. You can also choose to imagine a computer, an iPad or a tablet, and you can even see yourself using an Akashic Search Engine to find the information that you're looking for.

Some people say that the records are held in great buildings of vibrations, magnificent places such as the Hall of Records, or the Hall of Learning. You can visualize the place you visit in any form. It is your intention and energy that are the key factors in making this connection.

The meditation below will introduce you to one of the places that we will be visiting to tap into the record storehouse. It's your own Sacred Temple, and you'll be meeting one of your record guides there. This guide will have a bit of information or inspiration for you, so let yourself be open to receiving.

Exercise: Your Sacred Temple meditation

The following exercise is the script of a meditation process. You can either follow the steps in your own fashion or you can record it and use it as a guided visualization.

1. Get into a comfortable position and take a deep breath. Relax your shoulders, your arms, and legs. Let all the muscles in your body relax.

2. Take another deep breath. Release all thoughts and concerns and let your consciousness drift gently down into your heart center.

3. Relax even further and let yourself visualize a beautiful road ahead. You notice that the land around the road looks lush and green – filled with beautiful flowers and wonderful fruit trees. The sun is shining, and it's a beautiful day.

4. You now notice that further down the road, there's a stunningly beautiful building, your own Sacred Temple, shining so brightly in the sun. Perhaps it's made of bright white marble, crystal, or light-filled glass, shining there before you.

5. This is your own Sacred Temple, a magical place where you can connect to the Akashic Records and access all of the information you will ever need. You can also reach out to the spirit world, the angelic realm, your guides and masters, family, friends, and even your own higher self.

6. See yourself walking up to this beautiful shining building. Going in, you notice that it is filled with light and wonderful, loving energy. You feel a deep sense of peace, power, and happiness filling you up as you stand within this beautiful Sacred Temple of yours.

7. And as you feel that deep peace, you notice a brilliant light shining from the next room. Passing through the door, you see a beautiful spirit there. This is your guide to the Akashic Records, and you know

that this loving being is here to help you. Stop and make a heart-to-heart connection with this being, feeling such a powerful flow of unlimited love and abiding support.

8. You realize that this being has a message for you now. Open your heart to receiving this guidance. It may be just a word, a phrase, or even an image. Relax and take a moment to receive this message now.

9. You know that as time goes on, you will continue to get more and more Akashic information from this loving guide. Let yourself be open to whatever comes your way.

10. Take a moment to thank your guide for the love and support here in your Sacred Temple. This is the temple of your soul, where your Divine light shines and reminds you how valuable, deserving, and powerful you are.

11. Come here whenever you want to find your center, reclaim your power, or connect with the Akashic Records and with the loving spirit around you. This is your sacred place, filled with love and endless possibilities.

12. Let yourself remain peaceful now, as you come back to the present time and space, bringing the joy and knowledge with you.

13. Stretch out and bring your consciousness back. In the days, weeks, and months to come, you will be receiving more helpful information from the Akashic Field – through your intuition, the help of spirit, and through this process.

14. Continue to come back to this time and space. In the time to come, you will notice deeper and deeper connections with your guide and with other spirits, feeling the joy and guidance they bring.

15. Just let yourself come back slowly now, remembering your power and your ability to connect with the beauty, peace, and inspiration of this, your Sacred Temple.

The events of your present life are not your only history. Your eternal identity is a part of the mosaic of information that includes all the details of who you are, what you've experienced, and even what you may experience in the future. All of this can be unlocked. You have the ability to encounter eternity because you are already there. Your past, your future, your here and now are in the Akashic Records and are available to you. Your soul's map can show you where you've been and where your journey is heading.

By discovering all that the records have to offer, you open yourself to your soul's intentions. When that profound purpose is pursued, you will align yourself with the synchronicity of the Universe, and you will realize that every single moment in your life is filled with infinite possibilities.

SUMMARY

- ◆ Reincarnation answers many questions, such as why we feel connections to some people and why some patterns are harder to break than others.

- ◆ We return to Earth to gain new experiences that can help us learn and bring greater enlightenment to ourselves and to the world.

- ◆ Investigating our past records can help us to release negative influences and attract positive ones.

- ◆ The future exists in pure potential Our soul creates lessons for us, but our major life events are not scripted in advance, and they can be changed.

- ◆ There are many ways to open the record doors, including meditation, spirit messages, Akashic readings, spontaneous inspiration, intuition, and dreams.

Part II
ALL ABOUT YOU

*'You are led through your lifetime by the
inner learning creature, the playful spiritual
being that is your real self. Don't turn away
from possible futures before you're certain
you don't have anything to learn from them.
You're always free to change your mind and
choose a different future, or a different past.'*

RICHARD BACH, *ILLUSIONS*

Chapter 4

Connecting the Present with the Past

Your past is emotionally and energetically connected to your present, whether through childhood in this life or your experiences from previous existences. Understanding that connection is key to your personal healing and self-empowerment. As you view and rewrite your records, you can become more conscious of what you need to do now to create the kind of energy that will forge a desirable future destiny.

The word *karma* comes from the Sanskrit meaning *action*. The Akashic action you take now will yield dramatic results, both in your immediate life and in your far distant future. This energetic and timely connection is well worth investigating. Cause and effect reach from the long-ago past, through the present, and into the future. But the present is the door that leads in both directions, opening up information from the past and providing energetic shifts that lead to the future.

Portals of the past

An amazing amount of important information is stored in your personal Akashic Records, but you don't have to delve into the records themselves to start uncovering the old sources that are still influencing you today. Simply looking at your present life can reveal countless clues to past-life experiences.

In fact, this present-life investigation is a great way to get the process of record revelation going. As you take a look at your patterns from this life, your energetic action of investigation will open the portals of time and make the records more easily accessible. By recognizing the present-life issues that you want to work on, you will set the stage to receive all the past-life information you'll need for dramatic changes in those very areas.

Present clues to your unknown past

The following list contains some of the most common present indicators of past-life influences. An exercise after each section has a series of questions that can reveal which issues are most important to you now. Writing the answers will not only help to create access to the Akashic Records, it will also help create a readiness to receive specific past-life information that will be valuable in your record exploration.

1. Personal preferences, inclinations, or aversions

You may have noticed that you are called to a certain time or place. If you have a strong liking for something, whether it be the art, music, language, literature, or architecture of a certain place or era, this indicates a high likelihood that you had an incarnation during that time. And if you have a strong preference for certain types of climate or location, it's also likely that you had one or more lives in those types of locales. Interestingly enough, if you are repulsed by the food of a certain place, or if you dislike the fashions or music of a certain era, this could also indicate difficult or even traumatic past-life connections then and there.

On the other hand, if you are indifferent to a place or time, totally disinterested in its history, style, music, or cuisine, it's not likely that you spent any meaningful time there. It is the *emotional content* of your reaction that indicates the depth and the type of your past-life experience. Interestingly enough, your present-life ancestry can also be a karmic clue, indicating a high potential for you to have had a past-life experience in the places where your ancestors lived.

Exercise: Location investigation

Write down the answers to the following questions in your Record Journal to get some clues about your possible past locations.

✦ What are the countries of your ancestors – even the ancestors of your spouse or close friends? What countries have you visited – or would like to visit? Even if you have had to travel to certain places due to work-related commitments, that could indicate that you worked in those places as well.

✦ What kind of environment and climates call to you? Do you prefer cool mountain lakes, bustling cities, or arid deserts? What kind of climate or environment do you dislike or resist?

◆ List any notable likes or dislikes concerning such things as art, music, cuisine, culture, religion, or spiritual practice, and even clothing style. Look at each list – both the likes and the dislikes – and consider what era in history or place on the planet these preferences or aversions may represent.

2. Professions, talents, hobbies, and other interests

Your present job or career could also be a past-life indicator. When you engage in an activity on a daily basis for an extended period of time, there is a high likelihood that you've done something similar in the past. For example, if you are a teacher in this life, you may have been some sort of educator or even a nanny in a past life. Even if you hate your job, this may be a life of repetition for you, and it would be very valuable to investigate the records to find out the purpose of this occupational experience at this time.

Hobbies and other avocations could be past-life clues as well. For example, if you enjoy coin collecting now, you may have worked in a bank or even in a mint in a previous lifetime. And if you are a history buff, take note of the times and places where your historical interests lie. It's likely that your present passion places you right in the center of the historical events that you're interested in.

Your talents are also strong indicators. If you have an aptitude for learning languages, it's possible you traveled the world in a past life. If you like to play a certain instrument or even a certain sport, you will probably find the records of that in your personal history as well. If, however, you have a great deal of difficulty with something then that may indicate some significant challenges with that activity in the past.

A grinding experience

One client had celiac disease, an internal allergy to wheat, and when we investigated her records, we found that as a young man in a past life she had worked grinding the wheat to make flour – and hated every minute of it. The emotional charge of resentment actually attached her to the experience, forging a condition that she resents yet again.

Exercise: Interest and activity

Answers these questions in your Record Journal to open some past-life doors.

✦ List some of your favorite hobbies, talents, or preferred activities in this life. Also list the professions that you have engaged in (good or bad) or any jobs that you devoted at least six months of your life to. Consider the emotional content of these work experiences.

✦ What are some of the activities that you seem to have a strong or easy aptitude for? What activities do you find difficult or perhaps even uncomfortable in this life?

✦ Are there any careers or vocations that seem to have called to you and you have not yet pursued? Include any spiritual practices you may be interested in – or even resistant to.

3. Chronic physical, emotional, or financial problems or patterns

If you're experiencing a chronic physical problem, such as arthritis or allergies, it's likely that you'll be able to find its source in your Personal Records of the past. Medical issues such as heart problems, migraines, gastrointestinal conditions, and even cancer are often found to be linked to some sort of physical trauma in a past life. Even scars, birthmarks, and surgeries in this life can indicate past-life accidents or trauma.

Down to the bone

One client of mine had severe arthritis throughout his whole body from a young age. When we read his Past-life Records, we found that he was trampled in a stampede, and many of the bones in his body had been broken in that life, some of which had never healed correctly. That information was not only in his records, it was also being held in the energy of his cellular memory.

Ongoing emotional problems, such as depression, anxiety, neurological disorders, and even chemical imbalances can be a part of your Personal Records as well. Any addiction – which includes both physical and emotional components – would also be included in these types of patterns.

Even shared karma can have shared physical sources. Once in a seminar, a woman asked me what would cause many people in her family to have the experience of fibromyalgia in this life. When I viewed her records, I saw that she – along with the other members of her family who were burdened with this condition – were all in a mining accident, a cave-in where many died and others were seriously injured. When I identified the mine to have been in Wales in the UK, the women informed me that she was presently writing a book about a Welsh mining town in the late 1800s. She hadn't been aware of the fibromyalgia source, but she was clearly aware of her deep connection to that life and intuitively driven to write about it!

Your predominant emotions also carry record information. If you tend to live with consistent depression, fear, or anxiety, it's entirely possible that you've had one or more past lives where you had plenty of reason to be depressed, fearful, or anxious. Feeling powerless in this life can be a residual reaction to a lifetime where your power was taken away as well.

Out of service

I once had a client who was exceedingly shy and passive, always allowing others to dictate to her regarding the major and even minor decisions in her life. She recognized this pattern as being unhealthy – and as being a source of great unhappiness and restriction for her – and she longed to change it. In addition to setting up an action plan listing things she could do in her present life, we focused on this issue while searching the Akashic Records for its source.

What we found was a consistently repeated energy of servitude. In several lives she was a domestic servant, in another she was a slave, and in yet another, she was a lowly ranked wife in a harem of dozens of women who lorded their power over her. It was clear that this pattern was being repeated and this was the life where she was destined to take her power back. So she used the techniques in Chapter 6 (see page 110) to rewrite new records of those past lives. She also did affirmations to decode fear and self-doubt, and to reclaim her power and courage now. In addition, she worked on changing her behaviors and relationships in this life. She took more risks and engendered a more self-actualized and authentically empowered identity. In time, she felt more comfortable in her own skin and more powerful in her choices in life. She felt free!

Financial patterns can also be connected to the past. Even attitudes toward money that we learn as children can become a part of our records and influence us as adults. Beliefs such as, 'Money is evil,' or 'Life is hard, and getting by is even harder,' can be crippling. With these assumptions in your records, it can be very difficult to achieve financial success.

Present poverty can also indicate difficult financial patterns in past lives. If you've had lifetimes of fear or resentment of those who have money, that energy of resentment may keep you poor today. Or perhaps you've had a life that was filled with wealth and yet you lost it all. This is called a 'reversal of fortune' life, which creates deep records of fear and failure. This kind of financial trauma in a past life can record a compelling conclusion that money makes you a target or is easily lost. And though you may have a chronic longing for it in the present, you may also have a subconscious but very highly emotionally charged intention in this life to stay 'safe' by staying poor.

Exercise: Investigating problem patterns

Jot down your answers to the following questions in your Record Journal to see what impressions you get about your present patterns and their potential connections to your Personal Past-life Records.

❖ List some of the physical conditions that you've had to deal with in this life. Include conditions you may have had in childhood, for they could lead to past-life information as well. How have these conditions affected you? Have they led to any physical restrictions or created any emotional responses? Also consider any patterns that are both emotional and physical, such as addictions. Do you engage in any addictive behaviors? What would you like to change in order to gain more control in your life? There could be a past-life cause that you can discover and rewrite.

❖ What are the predominant moods you tend to live in? Do you have any chronic fear, depression, anger, or obsession? How do these emotional patterns impact your daily life, and are there specific people that tend to trigger such emotional reactions in you? This will be an important consideration when you're looking at relationship records.

❖ Are there any financial patterns that seem to be repeating in your life? Have there been long periods of lack or perhaps loss? What choices have you made monetarily that you would like to change – and which have you been unable to change?

4. Relationship patterns and lessons in relating

It's not uncommon for couples, families, and other groups of people to choose to come back to this earthly experience together. Not only do we want to repeat our loving relationships, we also want to work out the difficult issues that we've experienced with some of the people from our past. For this reason, our relationship records hold some of the most important information regarding the evolution of our soul.

The case of the lonely postman

A man came to see me about his inability to attract love. When we looked at his Past-life Records, we found he had a life as a pony-express rider – someone who rode horses to deliver mail to the farthest western reaches of the U.S. In that life he had fallen in love, but felt he shouldn't tie down the young lady because he was often gone for months at a time. So he determined that 'love wouldn't be right,' and he wrote that in his records.

He brought that conclusion into this life, and interestingly enough, he brought the profession, too. He delivered mail again, but this time he stayed close to home. He was able to release those old records and give himself the freedom to fall in love. Soon he met the girl of his dreams. With further research we found that it was the same girl he had left behind in that past life, and in fact, she even had the same first name!

The emotional context of our personal relationships often brings a lot of purpose and personal lessons to our lives. For example, we can become attached to others in a lot of different ways and for a lot of different reasons. Genuine love, of course, is a pure form of attachment, but there are other emotional energies in our relationships that keep us bonded to others in not so healthy or honoring ways – anger, resentment, and rejection just to name a few. So many of us simply react to the people in our lives, not giving it much conscious thought and not really caring what kind of records we are creating. Yet our relationship records can be some of the most powerful and influential energy sources in our lives.

When we're dealing with how we treat others – or how we allow others to treat us – it's a prime directive of the soul to bring a clear consciousness to it. And once we become conscious of the patterns we are engaged in, it's our ultimate goal to choose to honor ourselves and to demand it from others, no matter what the relationship may be. Let's look at some of the most common karmic relationships, and see what your present life may reveal about your Personal Records of relating.

Romantic love, spouses, sexual partners
The purpose of a loving partner is support, affection, mutual respect, and communication. If one of the partners is lacking in personal power or self-esteem, it may cause over-attachment, codependency, and potential lifetimes of repeated unhappiness. If one of the partners is abusive or hostile in any way, it could cause life after life of repetition or role-reversal.

When these and other problem patterns exist, it's up to at least one of the partners to recognize the opportunity for change and growth – and then to take some sort of action. Many people think that karmic relationships are destined to last a lifetime, but sometimes the lesson is just to learn how to empower yourself and finally let go.

Many people assume that a sexual relationship implies a loving relationship. This is not necessarily the case. Sex may be one of the most intimate energetic exchanges between two people, but it's not to be confused with love. And when one of the partners makes this misinterpretation when it's not the other's intention, this can lead to extreme feelings of disappointment and rejection – and clearly to lessons of self-prioritizing and self-valuing.

Parent and child

This relationship is one of the most energetically charged and one that can be filled with the most karmic lessons. The role of the parent is to love, guide, support, empower, and even help to inform the child of their eternal value and spiritual truth. If misinformation or mistreatment is rendered instead, it can create patterns of anger and retribution where the roles are switched and people treat each other meanly lifetime after lifetime. For children growing up in a hurtful environment of abuse, rejection, or dismissal, there are significant cognitive and emotional scars in their Akashic Records, causing unhealthy adult patterns that can drive a life forward in very difficult directions.

These records of negative treatment must be healed, with the emotions being ventilated, cognitions being reversed, and with new self-loving patterns being nurtured. In fact, there is often a key life lesson for many people that stems from their parental treatment – even if it's considered generally supportive.

*Ultimately, it's up to us to choose the beliefs
and self-talk that honor our eternal truth and
empower us on our personal path. No matter
what our parents taught us about ourselves
or the world, we are in charge now.*

This is an important truth. So when you answer the questions below, take a look at your present life – and use the techniques in Chapter 6 to look into your Past-life Records – to determine what patterns and responses to childhood you may still be carrying with you. Remember, you are likely to project them onto your adult attitudes and relationships.

Friends, siblings, and coworkers
When a relationship is healthy, no matter how intimate or superficial it is, certain things are required, including mutual interest, respect, and support. At the very least, any relationship deserves civil and, hopefully, kind treatment between both parties. The key to creating good relationship records – and healing any old negative karmic patterns – is honest communication, clear boundaries, and honoring self and others.

For some people it may feel risky (especially with family members) to set boundaries and insist on being treated with respect. But if these are not the parameters of your present relationships, it will be recorded in your shared karma and you'll likely have to come back and do it over again – at least until you make these goals a priority.

Isolation or the lack of relationships

This pattern of loneliness or isolation is often set in past records based in some difficult experience. If you've been hurt, abused, or abandoned in a past life, you may choose isolation now to stay 'safe.' Perhaps you took vows of celibacy or felt that isolation from society would bring you 'closer to God.' Or maybe there's an old fear of intimacy due to some past belief that you could lose power or control. All of these old records need to be erased and rewritten with attitudes of trust and openness to receiving love.

Your relationship with yourself

This may be listed last, but it's energetically the key to all other relationships in your life. As a result, an important present-life investigation is to explore how you treat yourself, what you think about yourself, and how you talk to yourself on a daily basis. These patterns are written in your records from way back and will continue far into the future, so it's extremely important to bring your intention and consciousness to them.

In consciously creating a relationship with yourself, you should focus on self-honor, respect, compassion, and priority. These approaches are the goal of the soul because they reflect a recognition of your eternal identity. Such karmic directives also show up in your relationships with others. And if these honoring approaches are at the core of your relationships, they make it easier to develop mutual respect and comfortable expression, as well as the ability to make reasonable requests and set healthy boundaries.

One of the main reasons we come here is to share this earthly experience with others in healthy, happy, and productive ways. Relationships – or the lack of them – are a central theme in our ongoing records. And if we want to make this part of our lives fulfilling, it will be important to set the records straight in our relationship with ourselves.

Exercise: Relationship investigation

Answer the following questions in your Record Journal. This may raise difficult feelings, but be honest, for your Relationship Records are key factors in your happiness and destiny creation.

1. List some of your emotional reactions to the following relationships in your life:

   – Parents

   – Romantic relationships, spouses, or sexual partners

   – Children

   – Friends, siblings, coworkers

2. Do you have any of the following emotions toward any of the people above? List the name or relationship according to each emotion:

   – Fear

   – Appreciation

   – Anger

   – Love

   – Rejection

   – Acceptance

   – Judgment

- Support
- Any unresolved negative feelings?
- Any unexpressed positive feelings?

3. How do you relate to yourself?

   - Do you give yourself the respect, priority, and encouragement that you would like to receive from others?
   - How do you treat yourself?
   - How do you perceive yourself?
   - How do you speak to yourself?

4. What do you need to change in your relationship with yourself? What do you need to do to be more self-honoring and supportive?

5. What do you need to do to create relationship balance and inner and outer harmony?

6. Consider your patterns of self-honoring regarding the following choices in each relationship, including that of yourself:

   - Self-expression
   - Speaking your truth
   - Setting boundaries
   - Reclaiming your power
   - Making reasonable requests
   - Releasing attachment
   - Releasing judgment
   - Engaging in compassion
   - Acceptance of self and others

Present clues are Present Records!

Remember your records are not just about your past. Every single moment you are recording energy and intention in the Book of your Eternal Life. How you treat and perceive yourself and others creates some of the most powerful and compelling energy in your records and your destiny creation. It is incumbent upon you to bring your awareness to this and every endeavor of your life.

Healing these – and any other unhealthy pattern – is a part of your soul's directive and a large part of the purpose of the records themselves. The Akashic Records are in no way a tally of your misdeeds or misinformed choices, something you'll have to pay back item by item. They are a vibrating representation of your history, your choices, and your priorities throughout your eternal life. And they bring you endless opportunities to understand, change, heal, and grow.

It is your soul's desire to change the records that don't honor you and to shift the vibrations that inhibit your genuine happiness. You can work on changing the negative records of the past, but your movement to a higher level of enlightenment requires you also to bring your consciousness to your ongoing Akashic Record-writing process.

Awaken your willingness to let go of old habits and to write beneficial new records in every present moment.

Whatever your present patterns may be, every present moment offers the opportunity of choice – choice of thought, behavior, focus, and priority. Let go of worry and self-criticism. Consciously record trust and present appreciation instead. Let yourself shift your negative emotions even for a little while, and you will be shifting the patterns that your records hold, bringing light and joy to the library of your eternal life.

SUMMARY

◆ Present-life investigation is a great way to get the process of record revelation going for two reasons: it helps to open the portal to the Akashic Field, and it helps to raise your awareness of the specific issues you'd like to work on in your record investigation.

◆ Personal preferences, your profession and talents, patterns of behaviors, and relationships are all potential indicators of past-life experiences.

◆ Predominant emotional and cognitive patterns, such as fear and self-judgment, are strong indicators of present-life lessons brought forward from the past.

◆ Present clues reveal Present Records, and you can bring your power of intention to the changes you want to make now.

Chapter 5
Records of the Past Revealed

Your Personal Records are vast. Your eternal soul glides on the currents of time, moving through centuries and individual personalities, yet maintaining its intrinsic spiritual identity. Within the consciousness of your soul is a record filled with information devoted solely to you – from the beginning of time to the present, and on into the limitless future.

Whether you're aware of it or not, your consciousness carries the codes that are written in your records from lifetime to lifetime, and your present life – this very moment – is being influenced by (and is influencing) your Eternal Record. Energetic vibrations, beliefs and conclusions, emotions and memories, all of these experiences from previous lives contribute to the resonant signature that is vibrating in your own unique record. These Past-life Records can be housed in your physical cells and in your life-force energy. Your eternal history – from the source of your spirit through every embodiment up to this very moment – helps to shape the person that you are today as well as the events and people that you're likely to attract in the future.

Your recorded karma

Life after life, your karma gets recorded. The code that is yours alone embodies who you are, what you've been through, and all of your responses to the events in your lives. These karmic records drive your energetic makeup. Your soul's intention to experience life is filled with the excitement of adventure and also with the desire for deep understanding, growth, and enlightenment.

Karma is not punishment, not a disciplinary action given to you from above. It's the soul's process of learning, evolving, sharing, and growing. Your karma may be written in the records, but it's not written in stone! It's your soul's unique design to help you shift into higher levels of consciousness.

Karma is an action with many purposes and lessons. Your energy patterns can be understood, returned, or exchanged to give your soul room for expansion. Understanding your karma allows for flexibility and movement of energy. These shifts and movements in the records – and in your present life – then influence your consciousness and, of course, your future. By learning the lessons and acting upon past and present patterns, you can bring healing to your life now, to the future in this life, and for lifetimes to come.

Past-life purpose

Reading the records of our karma can give us guidance in clearing up the messiness of our present lives. First, we can access past experiences to understand the energies involved. Second, the records can reveal vital lessons that are important for us as individuals, helping us achieve growth and loving enlightenment, as well as assisting in the expansion of love and enlightenment in the Universe.

The recognition of the intrinsic value of yourself and others is an important lesson and record directive for the action of your current life. This shifts your consciousness and writes new Present Records that will create happier results. These harmonic vibrations resonate with Universal action, opening the door to greater blessings and releasing the old karma that may have kept you stuck.

If, however, you resist the lessons that the records reveal, situations may be put into play that force you to deal with the required change. Keep in mind – there is no bad karma, just energy returning. You may face difficulty after difficulty, all of the same nature, not as some form of punishment, but as your soul's intention for change. But your willingness to look into the past and shift your behavior in the present would complete the lesson, rewriting your records and preventing more problems in the future.

Etched in the records

It is said that every moment – every thought, experience, and choice – is written in the Akashic Records. But some of these experiences have more power and, as a result, tend to become more deeply encoded than others. Some are far less significant and fall away in their influence. Yet others, like repeated personal connections, physical issues, or intense feelings can become dominant directives in your record patterns. There are the three types of influences that are likely to require rewriting in your own Akashic Records.

1. Highly emotionally charged events

Whether it's in a past, present, or even future life, the more highly emotionally charged an experience, the more influence it can exert on your thoughts, behaviors, feelings, career, and relationships. Whether an event is joyous or difficult, the greater the emotion, the greater the impact that event has on your experiences and on your perception of those experiences. An extremely pleasurable experience – such as love, friendship, passion, or joyous appreciation – will have great potential to influence your current life in a very positive way. On the other side of the coin, any profoundly negative experience, such as abandonment, financial adversity, severe illness, loss, or betrayal will wield an equally great influence in the opposite direction, significantly impacting your life experiences and choices.

Once the records have been written, they become a part of your energetic code, and until you rewrite those records – or create a different present pattern regarding the specific issues – those past records will maintain a pretty consistent influence in your life.

Karma blocking love

I had a client who had great difficulty finding love, and even when she found a relationship, it never seemed to last. Upon investigating her Past-life Records, we found that she'd had the same problem in several lives. She had recorded a deep belief that love was impossible for her, along with strong emotions of frustration and rejection. But she used the techniques in the next chapter (see page 110) to create new records and to turn those beliefs and emotions around, and in time she was able to find the love she was looking for.

You may also be seeking a solution to a highly charged issue yet having little success. But that could be due to the fact that you're unknowingly repeating negative emotions and beliefs from the past. If so, your present goals and desires are in conflict with a deep code that is etched in your record, one that is creating energetic obstacles that you may not even be aware of.

2. Health issues and physical traumas

As we saw in the last chapter, some present-day problems could be signals of body traumas from previous incarnations *(see page 62)*. These experiences are not only written in the records, they are also likely to be encoded within your cellular consciousness, creating an undercurrent of physical or mental disruption within your subconscious memory and your physical patterns.

Waterlogged

I once had a client who nearly drowned in a previous life and was suffering from asthma in her present life. She had a debilitating phobia of water and, of course, refused to go on boats, but she also had experienced severe anxiety, and even panic, when taking a shower or a bath. After working on clearing her fear and

rewriting her records her asthma was greatly reduced,
and although she had no desire to go boating, she was
now comfortable in the bath.

Many challenges that you face in this life can come from
the records of your unknown past. Physical abuse, mental
or emotional attacks, or even past-life accidents can
contribute to your physical experience in this life. Such
strong experiences in the records can become so deeply
encoded in your consciousness and your cellular memory
that they play a major role in your bodily experiences in
this life. Of course, not every physical problem is rooted in
a past-life source. But the threads that are connected to
your serious or chronic conditions can often be linked to
the highly charged physical events recorded in your past.

An extension of this truth can be seen in the recorded
information of past-life deaths. Both the timing and the
intensity of death can become a part of your record –
and a part of your present influence. If death is untimely
or abrupt, significant disruptions to the path of the soul
and its intended lesson could compel the spirit to return
immediately. That spirit comes back with the records left
intact upon his or her death – along with the emotional
and physical code that was created through the death
experience itself.

Fear of fire

I have a friend who had a dream that she had died in
a fire. Yet she could tell it was a past-life experience
because of the old-fashioned style of clothing. She then
realized why her whole life had been filtered through

a fear of fire. In fact, whenever she would travel, her
first activity upon checking in to her room would be to
investigate where the exits and fire escapes were.

Of course, death is an emotionally charged issue at any age, but when it comes to the young, it is especially compelling. The soul not only wants to experience life's pleasures, but also wants to complete its lesson plan for this time around. Youth by its very nature is very exciting and highly emotionally charged. When a life is cut short, it creates a compelling record directive, often causing the soul to long to rejoin the adventure right away.

Death coming during old age is less likely to be as emotionally charged, but there is usually still a desire to hold on to the glorious experience of life. But at this point, one's records are filled with a myriad experiences including love and loss, joy and sorrow. As a result, this soul is often ready to reconnect with its loving source. When the readiness to move on is much greater, the record of trauma or difficulty is far less influential.

3. Relationship patterns

As I described in the previous chapter, some of the most significant elements in the records of your soul are your patterns of relationship from lifetime to lifetime. These unknown records from your past may be a powerful force in your present. The relationships of a husband and wife, parent and child, friend and friend, are filled with countless events peppered with pretty much every emotion from deep love to extreme anger, from exhilarating joy to heart-wrenching rejection.

In answering the relationship questions in the previous chapter (*see page 70*), you probably saw some repeated emotional patterns that may be uncomfortable for you – and that you may want to change. If you haven't yet completed those investigations, I highly recommend that you do so before starting the exercises in the next chapter.

The records will also reveal important connections between the emotional patterns of your past relationships and intrinsic conclusions about yourself and others

Rewriting love

For example, one client who experienced chronic mistreatment from her parents in this life grew up to have serious doubts about her self-worth. Those doubts made her shy and retiring, and her adult relationships were pretty much non-existent. We found that these experiences were also written in her past lives, and they dominated her emotions and self-view in the present. She was able to rewrite both her Present and Past-life Records, and she used affirmations and other exercises in this book to change her history and her conclusions. It took some time, but she's now in a happy relationship, with a beautiful baby girl.

Your Akashic Records can reveal very specific information about the past-life events that are influencing the relationships, the physical issues, and the emotions that you're experiencing in this life. You can change your unwanted patterns from the past and reclaim the power of your eternal truth. In fact, if you want more strength, more ability to speak up and receive respect, if you want more autonomy, more freedom, or even just more peace or passion, all of these things are achievable when you learn how to rewrite the records of the past – and choose to create powerful records in the present.

When purpose piles up

Each and every lifetime brings a plethora of experiences that become the gateways to our emotional growth and self-mastery. Through this energetic process, every soul evolves – and brings specific purposes directed toward that evolution. The experiences that we learn from give us a road map, our soul's map, guiding us forward in our lives. As time flows on, our consciousness becomes more complex and our reactions become more layered.

It is part of the purpose of record investigation to peel back these layers and uncover our soul truth, bringing healing and recovery to previous pain or present difficulty – both for ourselves and others. In fact, it's the patterns of our present life that our soul longs for us to focus on. When unhealthy situations and reactions persist, it's a sign that we need to learn from past lives how to have the courage and strength to release our negative cycles. It's helpful, then, to understand what kind of causes keep our karma coming back.

Three main karmic causes

One of the reasons your soul chooses to incarnate is purely out of the desire to experience all the glories life has to offer. There are wonderful things to see, feel, hear, and do, and the soul is drawn to this earthly realm to taste both the sweet and the bitter. In fact, the soul longs for the adventure of it, and it's willing to experience all the colors and energies that the Universe sends its way.

But in addition to simple experience, the soul knows that each incarnation brings a great potential to learn and grow. Through the perception of the soul, our difficulties become opportunities, pathways to deep understanding and greater connection with our eternal identity. These opportunities come in the form of three major karmic causes, *repetition*, *compensation*, and *retribution*. These three karmic causes can actually become compelling, yet often unknown, forces in determining our destiny. And the Akashic Records will not only reveal what the specific influences are, they can also demonstrate what we need to do to change our unwanted patterns.

1. Karmic repetition

Since part of the reason the soul comes to this life is to experience pleasure, it also longs to *repeat* those pleasurable experiences. We are drawn to come back to feel the wonderful sensations of love, sex, music, food, art, sports, and all sorts of sensory enjoyment. As a result, we can come back lifetime after lifetime with the intention of joyful repetition.

Unfortunately, the karmic cause of repetition becomes an opportunity for learning and growth when the longing to repeat turns into *attachment*. We can become attached to such things as people, alcohol, food, sex, gambling, or any number of activities that may start out as simple pleasures but can turn into unhealthy addictions.

In fact, many present-life addictions are rooted in the repetition of past-life experience. The records reveal that when we love the feeling that something or someone brings to us, we often inscribe the assumption in our records that 'this makes me happy.' This assumption then becomes a driving force in our lives, even if the happiness is short-lived and the attachment actually leads to misery in the end.

For example, a person may enjoy drinking, and this pattern may start in this life in a very reasonable way. Yet this can, over time, lead to uncontrollable addiction, especially if there are records of many past lives where alcohol was a predominant force. Even if in some of those lives the pattern of drinking was healthy and in control, the repetition can accumulate and lead to deeper attachment and more profound opportunities for the soul to choose balance and self-mastery.

It's also entirely possible to consistently repeat things that aren't pleasurable at all, yet for some reason they are very compelling.

Records of self-love

One of my clients experienced this when she realized she had been an extreme people-pleaser in this life. She put everyone else first, to the degree that she not only sacrificed her own leisure time and happiness, she also eventually sacrificed her health. We discovered that this pattern was a deep part of her record, and as toxic as it was, it had been repeated lifetime after lifetime. It was now clear that her soul's directive was finally to learn

to put herself first and acknowledge her own value and
deserving in this life, releasing this pattern once and
for all. Not only did she use the exercises to rewrite her
Past-life Records (see page 110), but she also rewrote
her present patterns, mustering the courage to put
herself first and set boundaries with others. Although
it surprised others to see the change in her, she loved
the woman she had become, and she knew she had
changed her records for all of the time to come.

This is a big part of your karmic purpose, to stop repeating the patterns that are unhealthy or destructive to you, those that don't acknowledge or prioritize your soul's worth. Remember this:

Repetition is driven by familiarity and longing –
even if what you're longing for or familiar with
isn't good for you. If something doesn't honor
you, it's time to let it go. When honoring choices
and habits continue to drive you, your soul will
accelerate through lifetimes of learning into the
blissful enlightenment it longs for above all else.

2. Karmic compensation

This karmic cause occurs as an overreaction to extreme situations experienced in previous lifetimes. Difficulties, loss, or any perpetual problems could record a longing to move in the opposite direction, often to the extreme.

Like repetition, many addictions are born out of compensation – but for vastly different reasons. For example, if you spent a previous life in a constant state of hunger, you might come back and engage in the constant activity of eating. If you had a lifetime where you were constantly lonely and looking for love, you may come back in a life of compensation, experiencing many relationships and perhaps even sexual promiscuity.

Help wanted

I once had a client who had a horrible time getting and keeping a job. She would get rejection after rejection, and when she finally landed a job, she didn't keep it for long. When we investigated her Akashic Records, we found a lifetime where she had been a working man with a very large family. In that life she had to work three or four jobs at a time just to keep the kids fed. She was exhausted and resentful, for she never got to see her family. She constantly thought, I wish I didn't have to work so much. I hate all this work. *Her extreme activity and intense longing not to work brought her back to a life where she unwittingly got her wish.*

Any record of perpetual longing could bring back a life of compensation. In fact it's not uncommon to go back and forth from one extreme state to the other over and over again. For this reason, it's important to be conscious of your attitude toward your present experience. Let's say, for example, that you have a weight problem as a compensation for previously living in a period of famine and hunger. If your present attitude is filled with self-judgment and the desperate desire to be thin, you could come back in another compensatory life where you are anorexic or perhaps impoverished and unable to obtain food.

Where karmic compensation is concerned, remember this:

Any extreme imbalance can lead to a life of compensation. It is, therefore, important to work on creating balance in all the areas of your life, including your thoughts, behaviors, and daily choices. When given the option to focus either on longing and lack or on value and appreciation, gratitude will write better records and garner greater karmic results every time.

3. Karmic 'retribution'

The word 'retribution' may sound like some sort of Universal payback, but it's not. It's simply a return of your own energy, your soul's choice to experience something that you may have put forward in the past. In other words, if you had been hurtful to somebody, you might choose to come back and receive the same kind of energy and treatment from that same person in a different capacity in this life. It's not that you're being punished for your misdeeds, just that your soul wants you to know what that type of experience feels like.

The fact is, we can play these weird role-reversals with the same people over and over again, bringing similar energy to each other, yet merely playing different parts. This kind of jumping from part to part happens most often in romantic relationships and in the relationships of parents and children, but it can also happen in other relations, such as work or friendships.

Mistreating your own child – damaging their self-esteem and making them feel unsafe and powerless in the world – is a deep karmic cause. The child who receives this kind of treatment often responds with resentment and deep-seated anger. Both the resentment and the mistreatment are energetic causes for following lifetimes, causing the souls involved to come back together, either switching places or repeating it all over again.

The same can be true for romantic relationships. Criticism, hostility, or downright cruelty between two people who are brought together to love each other can record some crazy karma. The one who has been mistreated could come back with longing for that very person all over again, hopeful of finally receiving the love they didn't get the first time around. Or it could cause the couple to come back, switching places and grasping for power in any way they can.

Karmic retribution does not only take place in these kind of close and intimate relationships, it also includes your attitude toward other individuals and groups. Mistreatment, judgment, or prejudice are very hostile energies to perpetuate in the Universe, and they are bound to be recorded and returned to you in the time to come.

Your choice to look down on others whom you perceive as being less educated, less equal, or less worthy than you – for any reason – will reach into the records of your future lives. Your judgmental attitude now could set the stage for you to come back in the very same life circumstances as the people that you are presently judging. Where your karma is concerned, it's important to understand this energetic truth – that which you judge, you *will* experience.

Your negative view of others dismisses their soul value, which is the true source of their eternal identity – no matter what circumstances they may be experiencing in this life. This goes against the core of your soul's intention, which is to see the Divine value in everyone – both in yourself and others. The fact is, we all share a beautiful legacy, the Divine spirit of our loving source. In any life, in any identity, this connection is our greatest gift and our highest vibration.

Keep this in mind regarding every relationship – with yourself, with others, or with the world at large. Whether it's what you say to your spouse or what you think about another race or culture, the records will remember:

How you treat and view others now will be how you yourself will be treated and viewed in future lives.

Turning the tide

One of my clients used the following exercise to find the karmic cause of her own submissiveness and her husband's hostility. When the book opened, she saw a past life where she had been verbally brutal to him, constantly demeaning him. She realized this was a life of retribution and her soul wanted her to know what such treatment felt like. She learned her lesson, though, and determined never to treat someone like that again. She also realized her past-life patterns were either to shut up or to scream in hostility, so she decided to deal with her husband assertively and lovingly, firmly demanding the respect she deserved. She knew she turned a karmic corner when she was able to speak up respectfully instead of shutting down.

Exercise: Finding a karmic cause in your Akashic Records

The following exercise is a process that takes you to your Hall of Records. For the best results, spend some time planning which issue, relationship, or problem you want to determine the karmic cause for. Pick one item only and consider how you want to phrase the question, such as 'What is the karmic cause of my alcohol addiction?' or 'What is the karmic cause of my fear of heights?' Once you have your question in mind, simply follow the steps of the process and open up to receiving the information from one past-life event that was a precursor to the present issue you have in mind.

1. Take a deep breath and relax the muscles in your arms, back, and legs. Let all thoughts go, yet keep your karmic question gently in your mind.

2. Take another deep breath and as you relax further, let your consciousness drift gently down into your heart center.

3. Continue to relax as you notice a soft light glowing in your heart center. As you feel the peace of this light filling you up, you notice a stately building in front of you. Above the door is a sign that says, 'Your Hall of Records.'

4. Let yourself enter the building and look around you. You see tall shelves of books on each wall and in the center of the room is a tall wooden table or podium with a beautiful, large book on it.

5. You go to the table, look at the book and you see your name on the cover with the words 'Your Personal Records.'

6. These are the records of your eternal life, and they hold all the information of every thought, feeling, and event you've experienced. Just gaze at this book in calm appreciation, knowing that the wisdom and power of your eternal self brings information through this source.

7. Now consider the issue you're inquiring about. Remaining peaceful and relaxed, ask your question, and as you do, you start to notice the book open up, flipping to just the right page to answer your question.

8. You notice the book settle on a certain page. The page may have words written on it or an image floating above it. Let yourself see or sense whatever feels natural to you. Either way, this presents a source of the issue you asked about. Perhaps it's a complete event playing out, or perhaps the answer is a written explanation on the page. Just take a moment to get some details now. You may only get it in bits and pieces, but rest assured the information will fill in over time.

9. And now let it go. You see the print or image fading away, and you start to notice the pages of the book flipping again. The Record Book is about to tell you what type of karmic cause this is, and when the book falls open again, you will see just one word on the page, either 'repetition,' 'compensation,' or 'retribution.'

10. Let the book fall open now and see which word you get. Don't analyze, don't worry, just let yourself receive and accept. You may intuitively know what this means, but you will also receive deeper understanding about it as time goes on.

11. And now that you've received this last piece of information, you can let it all go. You know you can come to the Hall of Records any time. Your book is always here, always ready to inform and guide you.

12. So let yourself stretch out and come back to the present time and place, bringing the information, peace, and wisdom with you.

This exercise offers just a glimpse of a karmic cause to an issue that you're working on. In the next chapter there will be more techniques that you can use to shift any difficult pattern or relationship you desire. The beauty of the Akashic Records is that all the information you need is there. If there are past-life influences, no matter what the problem may be, you will be able to ascertain that influence and get information on exactly how to change things.

Even if you only want to take action in your present life, you can receive that guidance as well. You are a powerful entity who has the wisdom and deserving of the Divine within you. All the solutions you seek are held within the Eternal Records of time and space and in the records of your own eternal soul. Open your heart and mind to the endless possibilities waiting there – and to the many wonderful surprises your soul has in store!

SUMMARY

✦ Your present lifetime is influenced by your Eternal Records. Life after life your karma is recorded, revealing patterns in your energy, thoughts, and treatment of yourself and others.

✦ Karma is not punishment but the soul's process of learning, evolving, sharing, and growing.

✦ The more highly emotionally charged an experience, the more influence it can exert on your thoughts, behaviors, feelings, finances, career, and relationships.

✦ Each lifetime brings a plethora of experiences that become the gateways to your emotional growth and self-mastery.

✦ The three main karmic causes are repetition, compensation, and retribution.

Chapter 6

Changing Your Past Can Change Everything!

It's not uncommon that the Past-life Records we uncover often reveal difficult events, because those are the ones we are being called to heal and reverse. Each of us has many lives, however, where there was great joy. But it's the problematic past that needs to be rewritten so we can let go of what's negatively influencing us now.

Whatever it is you're going through, your eternal self is capable of removing the emotional blocks that are sourced in the past. Once you grasp the issues vibrating in your Personal Records, you're totally free to reshape the direction of your life. It isn't necessary to reverse every episode in your past. As you work on rewriting the main event, you can heal the issue and reverse unwanted patterns – even if they cross several lifetimes.

Though some patterns may take more time, the past, present, and future can often be altered in one brief moment. This powerful shift can redirect the power and energy of your present life, generating wonderful effects. With each new resolution, you become less burdened with the problems and difficult emotions of the past and move toward being more authentically empowered now. It's a process that's so illuminating and liberating, it can change the very nature of your life!

How it works

Stop and take a moment to reflect on your life. What patterns do you want to reverse? Is there something that you feel you're repeating or compensating for? Old, stuck energy can block the flow of your life-force vibration, creating obstacles to wealth, romance, healing, and even the creativity that you long for. But significant changes, like releasing present blocks, can arise when you rescript the energy, emotions, and conclusions still vibrating in your records of the past. Your consciousness creates both your records and your reality. When you clear the unknown yet influential experiences from past records, you shift your consciousness, and everything else starts to change.

Since all time is vibrating at the same time, it can be relatively easy to look into the records of the past and view some important events. It will be important, however, to create a focus for each viewing, one that opens the records to the source of the specific issue you're dealing with now. Once you've witnessed the event, you can rewrite the records of both the experience and the thoughts and emotions that go along with it. By changing those records, you can be released from the event and its influence. You can support that change by using affirmations in your present life and committing to *live* in the empowered energies that you chose in your newly written records of that event.

This is an important piece of your process – to support consciously the changes in your daily life. It may seem difficult at first. Habitual patterns can create a web of barriers. Feelings of fear, longing, or depression, although undesirable and unpleasant, can become a seemingly safe and familiar cocoon, one which sabotages your desires yet actually feels normal and protective. But you do have the power to let go and bring power, trust, expression, and worthiness into your intentions and your present circumstances.

It often takes courage to change the present, to take the next step, to move into the unknown. Yet rewriting your Past-life Records can be a significant help in the process. When you think of the simultaneity of cause and effect, you know that you can reach back and change the past, and in the very moment that you do, you are also shifting the future. Every moment is vibrating with pure potentiality – past, present, and future – and you can write brand new records in every area of your life.

Getting ready to view Past-life Records

There are two different meditative processes in this chapter, which are designed to help you take a look at the past and rewrite the records there. In the first one, you will view the records of a period of time just before the origination of the issue that you're focusing on. Although regression is probably the most common technique used to delve into past lives, viewing can be just as enlightening because you still have the awareness of both your present personality and the identity of that past life. You also have the ability to connect the meaning of that experience to your current situation.

It will be like watching a movie that you are in. You'll know who you were then and understand the details of the experience – as well as the thoughts and emotions of the person you were at that time.

Let yourself receive the information in any way that is comfortable for you. Although you are visiting a very specific episode in that life, you will be able to feel, sense, or recall everything that led up to that specific event. You'll also be able to recognize who the people are around you – if any. And you'll be able to understand their relationships to you both in that life and in this.

After you're done witnessing the event where the issue originated, you can stay in that life and proceed forward in time and see how the various elements in the situation played out then. This will be a helpful pursuit when you're doing the rewriting of the records of that life. For example, if you were attacked and robbed in the event, let yourself take the movie of that life forward. You may find that the injury of that event lead to a lifetime of pain, an experience that could be connected to a physical problem of this life. Or you may find that for the rest of that life you recorded the belief that it's unsafe to have money, a compelling record that could be connected to poverty in this life.

Choosing focused intentions for Past-life Records investigations

Poverty, illness, difficult relationships are all issues from your present life that you can focus on. But since the records hold *all* the information from your past lives, it's important to choose one issue at a time to view with the intention of healing. Here follow a few things you might want to consider when choosing your focused intention.

Reactive patterns

These are the uncomfortable emotional reactions that repeat in regular patterns in your everyday life, such as anxiety, fear of speaking up for yourself, feelings of inadequacy or inferiority; chronic worry or fear; depression or hopelessness. These are just a few of the patterns that could be sourced in your Past-life Records.

Unhealthy behaviors

Do you engage in any regular activities that are unhealthy or dishonor you? These could range from serious addictions like alcohol or drugs to simply feeling the need to work all the time. Any pattern of behavior could have its seeds in past-life experiences, and finding and erasing it in the records will help make it easier to change in this life.

Over-attachment

This pattern can manifest in a behavior, such as addiction, or it could be an attachment to a person or place, or an experience. If an attachment becomes unhealthy in any way, it could be very valuable to investigate it in your Past-life Records viewing. This includes relationship connections that no longer honor you.

Relationship issues

If you want to heal your difficult relationship patterns, rewriting your Past-life Records can be extremely helpful. Some common relationship problems include:

◆ Repeatedly attracting unavailable, critical, or dismissive partners

◆ Feeling stuck in dishonoring partnerships

◆ Inability to let go of old, lost love or longing

◆ Repeatedly finding yourself in hostile work situations

◆ Family history of being marginalized, hurt, or even abused; loneliness, isolation

◆ Lack of love

You can rewrite your past-life relationship records and give yourself the power and wisdom you need to change the energy of your present relationship experiences.

Records of responsibility

The search for empowered and truly loving relationships drove a client named Marie to look into her Past-life Records. Marie was in a cold and loveless marriage. She and her husband shared a home but not much more. She was a dutiful housewife who cooked and cleaned and worked hard in their home. Her husband implied that he needed her, but he never showed any appreciation for what she did. Marie was discouraged, yet every time she tried to leave, he made her feel guilty to the point where she would always decide to stay.

When we investigated this relationship in the records of her past lives, we found that her present husband had once been her son. Through an accident in a primitive type of kitchen, her son had lost his vision and his face had been badly burned. Throughout the rest of that life, Marie felt responsible for her son who never married and never regained his sight. Her records held deep guilt and relentless responsibility for him, and she came to this life with those feelings coded in her consciousness. The Akashic Records she brought with her from that life were highly charged with self-recrimination, grief, and also resentment for having to care for him day and night.

Marie's soul came to this life wanting her to take her power back. She had long needed to forgive herself for that experience – and to let go of responsibility for him. She came back with him to work this out and rewrite the records that had been keeping her stuck – in this life and probably in many others.

Once Marie made the connection between that Past-life Record of guilt and responsibility, she was able to understand why she had found it so difficult to let go. She was tired of the demands and the lack of appreciation, however, so she rewrote the records of that past-life event, erasing the accident and letting go of her guilt and responsibility. She saw her son in that life grow up healthy and able to take responsibility for himself, and now she knew it was time to let her husband do the same.

In addition to rewriting those records, she used affirmations of release and self-empowerment. In time, she mustered up the courage to take the action she had been longing for and yet resisting for so long. Soon she was ready to strike out on her own. When she finally did, she told me that she felt more liberated than she had ever felt before!

Tips for going back

During the past-life process pick one issue to focus on, but don't stress out over the details. The movie on your viewing screen will reveal an event in your Personal Records that took place just a few minutes before the origination of the issue you want to focus on.

Don't overanalyze the information you get. You may see or feel every vivid detail, or you may just get a vague sense of what's going on. Even if you don't tend to see or sense anything at all, your eternal consciousness is picking up some important data. So just let it sink in and repeat the exercise again, letting yourself be open to more and more information in the time to come.

Just as you shouldn't let any lack of information sidetrack you, try not to let any high emotions within the experience derail you as well. It can be uncomfortable to find out the difficult details of past lives. The experience you see may be very emotional and may have made you feel powerless then, but now the opposite is true. You're receiving the information so you can rewrite that record and move out of the experience that is the source of your present problem.

And if you find out that you behaved in an unkind way in a past life, especially if you were hurtful to someone you love in this life, make sure you stay objective. This can be very difficult, especially for parents who find out that they were cruel to the children they are devoted to today. But remember this is all a part of the eternal path of each person involved.

Never judge yourself for any mistaken paths that you may have chosen in your past. Understand that you were a product of the era, the culture, and your own personal history in that life. The reality is, you did the best you could do. And if you were wrong or mean-spirited, or even brutal then, you made the only choices that you could, given the parameters of all the circumstances of that life.

So forgive yourself! This process is intended to take you to a more empowered, more enlightened view of things, and self-forgiveness is an important part of your process. Things are neither good nor bad in your past lives. They are just a part of your eternal process, and it's what you do now that reaches back and forward in time and determines the energy of your eternal life. Responding to your lessons with grace, honor, and authentic power is your true achievement. Your self-love now – no matter what you did or didn't do in the past – is your energetic portal to clarity, understanding, and freedom in the present.

Exercise: Viewing Past-life Records in your Sacred Temple

In this exercise you'll be going to your Sacred Temple (see page 52) and your Akashic Record Screen, witnessing a past-life event that's connected to your focused intention. Simply follow the script, being open to any information on the screen and inspiration from your Akashic Records guide.

1. Just let yourself relax as you count backward from six to one. With each descending number you will feel yourself going deeper and deeper into relaxation, gently floating to your Sacred Temple, that place of special comfort, peace, and connection.

2. Six... relax all the muscles in your face, your forehead and eyebrows. Just let all the muscles there go loose, limp, and relaxed as you let go of all concerns and let your consciousness gently drop into your heart center. Five... your entire body is going deeper and deeper into relaxation. Feel yourself floating peacefully to your own beautiful Sacred Temple where you will be getting a glimpse of a past life in order to heal a present life issue. Four... a warm wave of relaxation is moving through your body. At the count of one you will be at your Sacred Temple, feeling so peaceful, so calm, and so comfortable there. Three... your entire body is deeply relaxed now. You feel a gentle peacefulness in your heart center and you're looking forward to connecting with your guide and getting an important look at a past-life influence. Two... continuing to remain calm and relaxed now, you will remain completely peaceful, calm, and relaxed throughout this entire process. One... you find yourself at your beautiful Sacred Temple, such a peaceful place, where you always feel welcome, calm, and relaxed.

3. As you start to see or sense yourself standing at the center of your Sacred Temple, you notice a beautiful light emanating from another room. You go in and find a wonderfully loving spirit there – perhaps

an angel or a guide. This is your guide to the Akashic Records, the storehouse of all the information you will ever need, including the potential experiences of past and future lives.

4. Take a moment now to make a heart-to-heart connection with your guide. You feel so relaxed and safe, knowing you will find out important information that will help you to release unwanted records and create greater healing and success.

5. You sit down in an amazingly soft and comfortable chair – it's almost like sitting on a cloud.

6. The guide directs your attention to the opposite wall where you see a screen appear. This is your viewing screen of the Akashic Records. You are about to view a glimpse of time from one of your past lives. Remember your intention is to identify the source of a present unwanted pattern and to see how this present life may be influenced by the past. Let yourself be open to the helpful information as the screen starts to come to life and you begin to see a brief little movie playing out in front of you.

7. Get your bearings as you see this event play out. Let yourself get a sense of the environment, the era, and the situation you're experiencing.

8. Take a moment to get a sense of who you are and what's happening to and around you in this brief moment of past-life time.

9. Observe things peacefully and objectively. Notice what's happening – and how you feel about it. If there are other people in the past-life movie, let yourself understand how you are involved with them. Get a sense of the connection there, and an understanding of how your present life has been influenced by that past life.

10. And now remaining in the life that you are visiting, take a few moments to let the movie go forward in time in that life. Find out what

happens to you – and perhaps to the other people in your experience. Allow the movie to keep moving forward in time until you find out the specifics about how that experience affected you in that life.

11. Take a moment to sense any thought or belief that you may have formed around this event. Sense how the experience made you feel about yourself or others. Become aware of any conclusions you may have made about yourself, your value, or your power then.

12. Get all of the information that you need. Let it rise up in your consciousness. And as you get some more clarity, you notice that you feel more comfortable and empowered now.

13. Take a moment to ask your Sacred Temple guide if there is any information they'd like to tell you. The information may come in the form of an image, a thought, a feeling, a phrase, or a word. Just let yourself receive it now.

14. After you receive this information, say thank you to your Akashic Record guide. Know that you will be able to meet with this guide whenever you desire.

15. You are now going to count upward from one to three. At the count of three you will be back at the present time and space, bringing with you a new understanding and a readiness to change. One... coming back to this time and space now. Your past-life influences are becoming clearer now. In the time to come you will receive more information and understanding about how that event is connected to your present life. Two... coming back to this time and space. You are always free to shape a new reality, write a new record. And your new understanding gives you courage and determination to reclaim your power in this life. Three... back to this time and space now. In the days, weeks, and months to come, you will remember to go to your Sacred Temple whenever you desire to relax, to connect with spirit, or to get any information from the Akashic Records.

16. Take a deep breath. Slowly open your eyes and stretch out. Put your feet flat on the floor and ground yourself. Feel the energy of the earth coming up into your feet, making you feel grounded, healthy, and happy.

This process can be very powerful, so let yourself experiment with it. If you don't get much information at first, repeat it. Also keep a notebook by your bed because once you open this investigation, you are likely to get more information in your dreams.

Speak easy

I once had a client named Dan who had a stutter, which was interfering with his potential advancement at work. He wanted to find out if there was a past-life source, so he used the exercise described above. What he saw on the screen was himself as a young man in an old-fashioned military uniform. He had been captured, however, and he was being interrogated in this past-life event. A brutal man was asking him questions, and each time he didn't answer, he hit this young man in the mouth. This happened for several hours until the man's entire face was crushed and his jaw was shattered. The entire time he was telling himself that he must not talk. His face and mouth were so disfigured that he had difficulty speaking for the rest of that life. Yet he had remained proud of the fact that his refusal to speak saved the lives of many men.

It was clear how the records of that event fed Dan's communication experience in this life. He had been determined not to speak and fearful that doing so would lead to disaster. He used the following technique, however, to rewrite that history and change the conclusions and emotions that had been written deeply in his records.

Getting ready to rewrite Past-life Records

The second meditation process utilizes the information from the first, allowing you to change and release the energy involved. You can rewrite the records of the single event and even of the long-term results experienced in that life. The purpose of this process is to inscribe new records of thought and emotion and to empower you in a situation where you might have been feeling powerless the first time around. By doing this, you will generate different vibrations, clearing old obstacles and creating new records that reach into this life.

The process is fairly straightforward. You'll go back to the viewing screen in your Sacred Temple. Then use the meditation in order to revisit and rewrite the event in question. This time you have all the power and control. Visualize the originating scene with a new outcome, one that empowers and supports you and leads to a happy and satisfied experience.

You can even make what may seem to be extreme changes to shift the event into a healthy and happy one, filling your new records with personal power. For example, if you were a child in the originating event, and you saw that you were being mistreated or harmed in some way, you can actually visualize yourself getting larger and gaining control of the situation. Tell the person who is being hurtful to you that they no longer want to treat you that way. See them respond with agreement and acquiescence.

Take some time in the rewritten record to experience and enjoy the new emotions you're feeling. Appreciate your new perspective – and your increased sense of strength, value, and personal resourcefulness. Let yourself create a record of all the new feelings – along with the positive beliefs and conclusions that go hand in hand with them. To do so, you can use predetermined affirmations or you can write them into your records at the time, using basic statements such as 'I am strong and self-actualized. I am powerful in any situation. I am worthy and valuable, deserving of love and respect.'

After affirming these changes, make sure you take a few moments to move forward in that life. Visualize yourself as a person who is self-directed, happy and empowered. See yourself living a long, healthy, and prosperous life before ending the rewritten record.

There are many options in record rewriting. For example, if you witnessed a past life where someone came up from behind you to push you off a cliff, you could turn around and inform the person that hurting you is not an option, visualizing that person leaving in total agreement. Or you could see yourself just step aside and they fall off the cliff themselves. Or you could see yourself having a meeting with the person before the event takes place, finding out what is at the source, and resolving the matter then.

However you turn things around, the action is intended to help you take your power back. The purpose of this process is to bring the qualities of your higher self, your Divine nature – which is always with you throughout eternity – into that experience. Connecting with your eternal wisdom, grace, courage, peace, and power changes both you and the experience at its core vibration.

You can use this technique to rewrite the record information that you receive in any modality – whether from regression, from readings or viewings, or even from dreams or other sources. You can also rewrite the records of any experience in this life. However, if you have had traumatic experiences in this life, you may need to rewrite those records a number of times and follow them up with specific affirmations that address the issue. The changes will take place, so let yourself rewrite it!

By rewriting the past, you erase the old record of fear and powerlessness. You strip away the attached emotions and false conclusions that went with that. This will reestablish your truth and remind you of the options that always exist for you. A new sense of personal and spiritual power will appear regarding all of your choices, experiences, and relationships in this life and in all the time to come.

Exercise: Rewriting Past-life Records in your Sacred Temple

You are going to go back to your Sacred Temple and to the viewing screen of your past lives. You can revisit the scene you want to rewrite, but this time you will be able to see the scene unfold exactly as you wish, with a more beneficial and empowering outcome for you. So take a few minutes to prepare a new narrative to reframe the entire event. Consider the action that would give you more power and a greater sense of your own value. Consider how you want to direct it to create a beneficial and empowered outcome for you.

Just let yourself relax and know that you are writing new records of personal strength, positive thinking, and joyous feeling.

1. Relax and take a deep breath. You're again going to count backward from six to one, gently moving to the light and love of your own Sacred Temple. At the count of one you will be at your Temple and meeting your guide. You will be able to view the same experience, same place and same time that you visited before. This time you will be empowered. You will be able to rewrite the record and direct your own reality. Just relax and go deeper and deeper into relaxation with each descending number.

2. Six... let your whole body relax. Let all the muscles in your arms and legs relax, and just let everything go. Gently let your consciousness float into your heart center.

3. Five... relaxing even further. At the count of one you will be at your Sacred Temple rewriting the situation and creating a different outcome and a very different approach than before.

4. Four... you can tell the people in this experience how they will treat you. You can change any part of the experience you want. You are the one that directs the experience now.

5. Three... your whole body is relaxed, moving safely and purposefully to your Sacred Temple now. You are in charge. You have the power now.

6. Two... at the count of one you will be able to redirect the event with self-empowerment, happier results, and more beneficial Personal Records.

7. One... remaining calm and relaxed, back at your beautiful Sacred Temple now. Your guide is with you, showing you the viewing screen. Let the screen come to life and see the event you want to rewrite. This time you have power to make any change you want. People

respond to you differently, and you respond to them differently. Take a moment to consider all your options. You choose how you want to go through the experience, and you notice that things are happening differently. You are in charge.

8. Let yourself see the scene taking place in a way that empowers and honors you. You feel so strong and so good about how things are going. You feel so empowered.

9. Take yourself through the situation, but this time the outcome is such a good experience. You have the power to write a new record, a new truth. Let yourself smile a little as you see yourself going through this wonderful, positive outcome, completely empowered and happy.

10. Take a moment now to move forward in that life. You see yourself living a long, healthy, prosperous life, one where you are happy, empowered and in control, experiencing all the joy and achievements that you desire.

11. And now let yourself take a moment to create a new belief. You are authentically empowered, peaceful, and serene. You are valuable, in control, happy, and free. Affirm and record these truths. Feel all of these wonderful feelings coming up now, vibrating in the records of this new experience.

12. You are valuable. You are powerful. You are deserving and self-directed. All of this is recorded into your consciousness, into your cells, your understanding, and the records of your eternal life. Just let yourself feel all of these positive energies now.

13. Bring these feelings of strength and power to this present life and to this very moment, as you slowly come back to this time and space.

14. Counting upward from one to three now. At the count of three you'll be back to this time and space with a new record of that past

life – and a new belief in your present consciousness about your authentic power, your true value and deserving. You feel healed, whole, healthy, and renewed, filled with a sense of your eternal strength and peace.

15. One... coming back to this time and space now, bringing back a wonderful, self-loving belief, knowing that it's a part of your consciousness and your Eternal Records. You have released the negative influence of that past life, and you've charged your Personal Records with power and joy.

16. Two... coming back to this time and space. No matter what you did or did not see, your eternal consciousness has made great changes here. You have reshaped a new reality, and you know that you can create this power in all of your present circumstances.

17. Three... in the days, weeks, and months to come, you will receive more inspiration and information regarding these changes; and your sense of empowerment will grow and grow.

18. Coming back to this time and space. Stretch out and breathe deeply. Slowly open your eyes, remembering everything. You have created new Personal Records, erasing the old negative records and replacing them with self-love, self-direction, and a deep sense of your own eternal power.

Dan used this process to rewrite his past-life experience and change the energy and conclusions around his present issue of stuttering. When he witnessed the new event playing out on the screen, he saw himself escaping capture and moving safely through that conflict. He saw *that* life moving forward in health and happiness, with him being able to communicate comfortably in any kind of situation.

He also used some of the affirmations below to reinforce his new beliefs. He learned how to relax with his own self-expression in the present. In fact, he hadn't realized how much anxiety he had been carrying around regarding this issue. It took some courage and determination, but he now knew that the source of the problem was a trauma that no longer had to affect him. With time and continued choices of self-empowerment, he was able to release his pattern of chronic stuttering. His affirmations of comfort and freedom became a reality for him.

Affirmations for past-life clearing and present empowerment

Whether it concerns a past life or a present circumstance, heartfelt affirmations can move your healthier intentions forward. Don't just pay lip service to your new ways of thinking and feeling. Use the following affirmations and create your own as well. Meditate on their meaning, breathing in the energy of their truth. Let yourself feel and experience the beneficial emotions and empowerment they bring.

Releasing affirmations

- ✦ I release the negative energy from any difficult experiences of the past.

- ✦ I let go of any toxic conclusions I may have made as a result of those experiences.

- ✦ I release feelings of powerlessness or any other difficult feelings based on those events.

- ❖ I have free will, and I make my own choices. I no longer need to respond according to any old hidden intentions. I release them and let them go.

- ❖ I release any toxic feelings or conclusions that I may still be carrying now.

- ❖ I release any physical effects I may have carried forward into this life and my current body.

- ❖ I release any toxic attachment to any person, habit, or situation – past or present.

- ❖ I bless the past and let it go. I am free.

- ❖ I am free and clear of any past imbalance or misinformation in my body and my mind. I live in my power and my eternal truth.

Empowering affirmations

- ❖ I open myself to my spirit's capacity to embrace the full measure of my peace, value, and power – now and always.

- ❖ My body is healthy, vibrant, grounded, and energetic. Divine Consciousness fills every cell.

- ❖ I open my heart and mind to a deeper connection with my spirit. I awaken to my Divine Source and identity more and more each day.

- ❖ I open myself to my spirit's capacity for knowing how to attract and maintain loving relationships – and fulfilling and prosperous careers.

- ❖ I forgive all karmic debt and ask that all my karmic debt be forgiven.

- ❖ I engage in healthy thoughts and choices, and I forge honoring relationships with myself and others now and forever.

- ❖ It is safe and comfortable for me to [*insert your intention here, for example: express myself, speak my truth, heal, love, be loved, trust, connect with spirit, etc.*].

- ❖ I open myself to the free and full expression of my power, value, and truth in every situation.

- ❖ Divine energy moves through my eternal life, releasing the past, healing the present, and blessing the future.

- ❖ From now on I choose freedom and self-empowerment. Each day brings greater enlightenment, purpose, prosperity, and love.

- ❖ I am open to the changes my soul desires. I live in the peace of my eternal perspective, and I know I am blessed.

Use these affirmations – and others – to write new truths in your Eternal Records and to help you apply their energetic changes to your present life. This is crucial to learning the lessons and clearing the problem patterns completely from your records. In addition to the affirmations, there are many other things that you can do to apply your new records to your daily life

Applying your new records to your daily life

Once you do your Akashic investigation and rewrite the records there, you have the opportunity to completely redefine yourself and your life. The reversal of every single past-life episode is not at all necessary. All you have to do is learn the lesson, and your new awareness – combined with new thoughts and behaviors – erases the karma from your Eternal Records. So in order to get rid of any residual negative energy, it will be important to support your new records in your ever-present choices and your self-talk. You *do* have the power in your life. It's time to believe that and start living in this truth.

For example, if you have rewritten the Past-life Records where you were submissive, never making yourself a priority, it will be your soul's directive to make yourself a priority now. If in the new records of that life you saw yourself standing up for yourself, making your own choices, and putting yourself first, those changes should be integrated into your present approach as well.

This may feel risky and very foreign to you at first. You've been living a certain way for a long time – perhaps even lifetimes – and you may be resistant to the changes. Yet this is the very purpose for rooting out unhealthy and dishonoring patterns, whether past or present, to lift the energy of your eternal life force and to rise to the level of peace and enlightenment that your soul longs for you to achieve.

You do have the inner strength to change your thinking, to change your behavior, to take action, and to be optimistic. These are all Present Record choices. Bring your consciousness to the real power you have to record joy and value in every present moment. This is the next, and perhaps most important piece of your Akashic Records creation!

SUMMARY

- ◆ You can view specific Past-life Records by choosing to focus on a present-life pattern or issue that you would like to change.

- ◆ By rewriting the records of a past event, you can generate different vibrations, clearing old obstacles and creating new records that bring happier experiences into your present life.

- ◆ The regular use of affirmations can help to release the past and set new intentions for the present and the future.

- ◆ Your choice to apply your karmic lessons to your present life not only shifts old karma, but creates wonderful records of honoring and empowerment now and in the time to come.

Part III

A UNIVERSE OF INFORMATION AND OPPORTUNITY

'If you want to find the secrets of the Universe, think in terms of energy, frequency and vibration.'
Nikola Tesla

Chapter 7

The Incredible Power of the Present Moment in Record Creation

Every single moment you are pouring information and energy into your own personal Akashic Records. Your thoughts, your behaviors, your emotions at any given time are being written in the records of your life. Some people say that you shall be held accountable for each and every choice, but that seems far too punitive – too much like a future trial passing down a condemning verdict – to represent the truth of what is going on. The accountability can be found more in your soul's intention than in some Universal court.

It's the accumulation of your personal energy, consciousness, and choices that sets you on the path of learning. Your soul wants to move to a higher vibration and live a life that is conscious, honoring, and enlightened. A big part of the purpose of your Personal Records is to allow you to bring your intention to your higher goals, to heal the past, program the future, but most especially make better choices about what you want to record in your present.

In fact, the present is your best and only time to take action in any direction, whether it is spiritual, personal, or professional. Your Akashic Records contain all of these directions, and many more.

Every single moment you are writing records and creating energy. Every moment you are living in some sort of consciousness – even if you're unconscious about what that may be. The profound power of the present moment is always within reach, and it's up to you to take a look at what you're writing now.

The records live in natural law

I have been teaching the principles of manifestation and Universal Law for more than 20 years, and I firmly believe in the creative power of energy and consciousness. But it wasn't until I started investigating the Akashic Records that I realized the extent of the creative force we wield in every moment of our lives. It becomes a very compelling motivation then, to think about our energy and consciousness in terms of our Present Records creation.

This is not just an ephemeral, abstract concept, but a clear act of setting down present vibrations in an energetic biography, a record of cause and effect that speaks our truth and reveals our potential consequences. Knowing this, the drive for unconflicted thought, peaceful and joyous emotions combined with conscious and intended self-mastery then becomes a primary focus in our lives. The understanding that we are always in the process of writing our Personal Records is a compelling reminder of our ongoing power of manifestation, influence, and creation.

*Your consciousness creates your
records and your reality.*

Your consciousness is a force in the world, and that makes you a powerful force yourself. In spite of this truth, very few people take the time to consider what they are conscious of on a daily basis. Most people consider their lives to be a series of random situations that they simply have to deal with. But the truth is, their consciousness moves out into the Universe, scripting many of the events that they are likely to experience. What you tend to focus on, what you expect on a day-to-day basis, even what you tend to think about most – all of these things indicate your consciousness direction and your record creation.

If you tend to focus on what's wrong with your life, then that goes into your Personal Records and into your consciousness creation. If you tend to think about what's missing – expecting poverty, mistreatment, or dismissal – that also goes into your Present Records and your consciousness creation. In essence, you are writing the play and yet wondering why the scenes are not to your liking.

But if you tend to focus on all the wonderful things in your life, that consistent focus will script more wonderful things to experience. If you tend to feel grateful, consistently acknowledging what you already have, that consciousness will write a record destiny where you continue to manifest even more to be grateful for.

So get up every day and take a moment to consciously write the expectation of happiness in the day to come.

Then make a concerted effort to record happiness in your thoughts, emotions, and experiences. Remember that the future is full of endless possibilities, and if you bring a joyous, trusting, and grateful consciousness to your record creation today, you will reap the rewards of countless happy sensations written in the records to come. After all, your Present Records vibrate with your own personal energy, moving outward in all directions, sending out signals of who you are and what you really expect.

Your energy expands and attracts

You are an energetic being, and you are constantly creating, transmitting, and receiving energy in the world. In fact, you have your own Personal Energy Field, a signature resonance that moves outward into space and time, connecting with people and situations of similar resonance. Eventually those people and situations will be drawn into your life in very real ways, filling in your Personal Records and influencing the ultimate direction of your life.

There are two major elements that contribute to the resonance that you are constantly broadcasting. They are the vibrations of your feelings, or your emotional energy, and the vibrations of your thoughts, or your cognitive energy. These are inextricably connected, for it's largely your thoughts that create your emotions.

Your cognitions are constantly sending out vibrational messages about you. Thoughts of self-criticism, worry, and fear are the biggest energy busters, and they write records of negation and doubt. Such thoughts will also create chronic emotions that poison your energy field and darken your record creation, not only now but in future momentum as well.

If you tend to live a happy and joy-filled daily life, your emotional energy records expectations of increasing bliss. If, however, you tend to live in chronic anger, fear, or dread, those energies will fill the records of your present life, rolling out volumes of the same in the future. And if such emotions go unchecked, they can expand into profound sadness or depression in Present Records and utter hopelessness about your future.

But you have the power to shift your present experience and change your records in remarkable ways. The truth is, the quality of your emotional life is up to you, and the Universe will respond to your higher intentions and healthier energetic choices. Greater love, happiness, and success will come back to you if you establish such things in the records of your life now.

One key to a brighter record creation is a positive perception of yourself and the world. Let go of self-doubt and choose to encourage and believe in yourself, even if it seems foreign to you at this time. You deserve your own high regard, and if you don't give it to yourself, self-love and respect will be missing from your Present Records, and that sad story is bound to continue.

It's also important to look at your future and the world as safe and even exciting. Choose to make choices and take action on your own behalf. Look at the world around you and see all that there is to appreciate and enjoy. Know that you are strong and capable of making your goals and desires a reality. These are the records you really want to live in!

The Universe is a friend of yours, and it wants to serve your intentions. So create the intention to experience – and record – happiness every day. Choose a joyous attitude toward your tasks and peace in your perceptions. Open yourself to the light and love that are already vibrating within the Eternal Records of your beautiful spirit. These daily intentions will focus your energy, revealing true happiness in your Personal Records now and creating it in the time to come.

Intention focuses your energy

You live with intention every day, and you record those intentions in your present-life story. Whether they are honoring and fruitful or dishonoring and self-sabotaging, those are different stories. You always have the opportunity to create a clear emotional intention about everything that you do. You can eat mindlessly or joyously. You can work resentfully or enthusiastically. You can get up dreading the day ahead or planning when and where you might be able to insert some excitement and fun. All of these are *emotional intentions*, and they affect your energy and consciousness significantly. But if you continue to follow the path of least resistance, you will continue to live in emotions, habits, and unconscious records that have their own momentum – whether they are healthy, honoring, or beneficial to you or not.

It's clear that in order to create vibrant and healing records, we must bring our consciousness to our intentions and habits every day. We have the option to create beneficial intentions and live in the emotions that we desire to focus on much of the time. We have the option to get out of our unconscious habits and create clear intentions in every Present Record – even in the time that we usually dismiss as being unimportant. Every moment is important. Every minute gets filed in our records. It's what we choose in the present that moves us relentlessly into the future.

Present choices for future results

It's an energetic truth that the ongoing choices we make in our daily lives accumulate to project our predominant personal resonance out into the future. It is, therefore, extremely empowering for us to be aware of our daily patterns – and to make conscious decisions about the kind of records we are creating today.

All too often we fall into unconscious thoughts, behaviors, and even emotions that are actually writing our Future Records without understanding or awareness. When we look at our records of the present, we can find out exactly which of our patterns are building the biggest momentum of our lives.

Investigate your records to determine what present patterns need to be changed. Always remember the multidimensional aspect of your energy production. It's your whole life force that moves out into time and space to forge your destiny. So consider all the elements of energy and consciousness creation when you do your Present Record investigation. Here are the most important ones:

Present records of thought

While it has become a cliché to say, 'Think positively,' it's far easier said than done. Yet, of course, there are lots of things to think positively about. To start with, *you* should be at the center of your positive thinking, allowing yourself to live with a self-view that is both loving and encouraging. This is a core element of your Present Record Creation:

Everything revolves around how you write yourself.

Something that you can do to change your thought records is to change your language. The words we use are so powerful; they script our entire lives. And they are certainly written verbatim in our records.

Fortunately, our words are something we can control when we set our minds to it. This is a matter of consciousness and choice. For example, there's a huge difference between the phrases 'I'm scared' and 'I'm strong.' Each could be used in response to a difficult situation, but the second is the most empowering and would clearly create the best records.

'I'm strong' is a simple yet powerful declaration that speaks your truth and informs you of your emotional options at a time when you may need to be reminded. In fact, there are many declarations that you can use to lift your energy and set yourself on a new path in any present moment. To assist yourself in this intention, I highly recommend the book *Power Words* by Sharon Anne Klingler, which has countless techniques to change your record language and to charge your life with higher vibrations.

Since your records are written in phrases, images, and energetic vibrations, giving power to your words is a great way to write (and right) the records of your life. This includes your thoughts about others, your environment, your work situation, and the world itself. Peaceful thoughts generate peaceful emotions, another important way you write your Present Records.

Present records of emotion

Together with your thoughts, your emotions are the strongest components in both your record creation and the quality of your life. That emotional quality speaks volumes about you, so it's important to look honestly at the present emotional records you're writing.

Living in dread, hopelessness, or chronic frustration clearly etches a far different emotional record than fun, optimism, and joyous expectation. But no matter what life has dealt you so far, it's important to know that you have the power to live from your heart and know that good things can and will come your way – if you choose to look for the good that has already come your way and consider the potential for happiness in every day.

Always remember, you *do* have the power to change your thoughts, and thereby change the emotions in your Present Records. The quality of your life is created minute by minute and day by day – not in the big or special events that you may be hoping for, but in the little everyday moments, in the choices of appreciation, relaxation, happiness, and hope. Where your Akashic Records are concerned, each choice to navigate the options of trust, faith, and peace of mind is a defining moment for you.

Present records of behavior

What do you do every day – and how do you do it? There are certain things that each of us do each day, like eat and sleep, maybe watch some TV, read the newspaper, get on the Internet, and text or communicate with friends and family. These are all behaviors that are a part of our everyday lives. For some, other things such as exercising, meditating, listening to music, and gaming are added to our daily repertoire.

How much, however, do you bring your consciousness to these activities? Some of these things are done without much awareness at all, such as eating – and perhaps overeating. But a *lack of consciousness* in your daily behaviors creates almost as much momentum in your records as your thoughts and emotions do. And the power of your unchecked behaviors can build like a rolling river heading toward the roar of a pounding waterfall, waiting to pull you down somewhere in the records of your future.

So take some time to consider the patterns of your behavior. You don't have to be perfect, but you do have to start evaluating what behavioral choices honor you. Then muster up the courage, strength, and self-mastery to make the honoring choice. When you do this on a consistent basis, you will find vastly different record results than if you had persisted in unhealthy present behaviors.

Present Records of action

Of course any behavior you engage in requires some sort of action, so in that way these two items are related. It takes action to exercise, to eat healthfully, to choose optimistic thoughts, and to spend your time in a beneficial way. These and many more present actions need to be chosen when creating wonderful Present and Future Records.

It would be impossible to achieve your goals without taking step-by-step action in their direction. Whether you want to build a business, make a sale, or write a book, certain steps have to be taken all along the way. Your action might change depending on the type of goal or the phase that you're in, but you are likely to need real, consistent action nonetheless. If you want your Future Records to say 'success,' your Present Records must read 'action.'

Your soul came here with specific intentions. Healing, peace, love, and self-mastery require specific actions, too. You also have a unique gift that you alone can bring to this life. Maybe it's service or scientific discovery, artistic creation or entertainment. Perhaps it's something more personal, like being a wonderful parent. Whatever your purpose is, make sure you take some action toward it now. To see the results of achievement in your records to come, write records of present action now.

Present Records of spirit

You have an eternal identity. That part of you that chose to come to this life experience is a major source of your energy production. In fact, it can be the strongest part, and it can write records of unlimited power. The problem is that most people don't see this wonderful side of themselves, nor do they turn to it when working on their personal life or their goals.

There's a whole world of power available to you in the energy of your spirit. If you learn to utilize that power now, you will energize your present and accelerate your ability to create an undeniably dynamic destiny in your future reality.

Your soul knows no limit of time. Your spirit can traverse space and eternity in the blink of an eye. It's easy for your spirit to go forward, to plant the seeds of your future in the energetic realm, and to write your desired results in the Universal Records. When you bring the records of your spirit to every moment and every intention, you make anything possible!

Recording your energy in the present moment

Your spirit has a much larger and longer perspective on life. Your soul does not see your problems as difficult or even troublesome. It sees these events as a piece of the mosaic that creates the pictures of your Eternal Records. The soul's vision sees the finer nuances that make up your present life. The beauty of a golden sunset, the caress of a gentle breeze, the fragrance of a blossoming rose, the music in a baby's laugh, and the bouquet in a sip of wine, all of these are just some of the events that your soul basks in with deep appreciation. While you may tend to focus only on the tough stuff, your soul sees every piece of the experience we call life from a far different point of view.

Each and every moment is brimming with life and possibility. Joy is a blessing and adversity is just another opportunity – even adventure – in the span of life. The soul's intention is to enjoy the pleasures that it appreciates, but also to utilize the powerful opportunities available at every moment – good, bad, or in between. And the reality is that you are writing your records in every experience, in every present moment, and those Present Records roll into your future realities, now and for lifetimes to come.

So many people dismiss the present while they're waiting for something special to happen in the future. Yet the truth is, the real special time is now, the most special moment is here. This is the moment that you have the power to choose – to choose what you think, what you feel, what you believe, what you do. It's all within this precious, powerful moment, and even a little shift in your choices now can create dramatic changes in your Eternal Records. For in every moment, no matter what may (or may not) be going on, there is always the presence of unending *adjacent possibilities*.

Finding your adjacent possibilities

In science, nature, industry, and even economics, the Complexity Theory demonstrates how various systems form and evolve over time. Within this theory there's a concept known as 'adjacent possibilities,' which reveals that at any moment, even a slight change in the process or the environment can take the entire system in vastly different directions.

Believe it or not, this applies to you, too. You have endless adjacent possibilities, and countless options at any moment. Even minor changes in any given moment can take your life in a brand new direction.

No matter what's happening, your life is special, and it's expressing itself in every single minute. How you respond to it is up to you. You can create a different thought, choose a new behavior, and write a different record. This, of course, calls for you to bring your consciousness to the present, even in the most mundane activities.

In fact, it's the routine moments that fill our records the most. Our daily emotions and responses usually become unconscious habits. If we get caught in traffic, we can get frustrated, or even angry. But we have many adjacent possibilities sitting in the very next moment. We could stay in our anger and frustration, or we could take a deep breath and relax. We could put on our favorite music and sing along or glance at the environment around us and take pleasure in the colors of the sky. We could recall a happy memory, think about a favorite vacation spot, or smile at the thought of a beloved friend or family member.

These are just a few of the adjacent possibilities that are available to you at any time. When you make an alternative beneficial choice, you change your energy, your records, and even your life. Remaining conscious of these options – and building new habits around these honoring and peaceful possibilities – will immediately create new joyous records for you now, leading your Future Records in surprising new directions. And even the little momentary changes can be connected to big events.

For example, your Personal Records at this time may indicate that you're likely to stay at your present job for the rest of your working life. But that could change. What you're doing, thinking, or feeling right now – the record of this moment, this hour, this day – could have the power to change that outcome to a lesser or greater degree. Almost everything depends on your present energy direction. Your new Personal Record is written out of your consciousness and energy shifts, creating results that may not have seemed likely based on your energy from just a few days – or even hours or moments – ago.

Think about it. The power in this truth is utterly liberating! You can take hold of your thoughts, your self-talk, your choices, your actions, and even your emotions right now. Change your Present Records right now – and your future destiny, too.

A moment changed, a life rewritten

I taught the following technique of writing Present Records to a client of mine named Shirley who used it to change some significant issues she was experiencing due to menopause. In addition to dealing with a weight gain of about 30lb (13.5kg), which seemed impossible to get rid of, she was also experiencing some very difficult bouts of depression. This was something that she had been unaccustomed to and there were times when it was totally overwhelming to her.

She realized that she was creating Present Records of chronic depression and unhappiness, and she knew that energy would lead to Future Records containing more of the same. So she started to ask herself, 'What do I want to record in this instant?'

Just asking herself this reminded her that she did have the option to shift her focus and take control – instead of riding the familiar wave of depression. She was determined to use the power of adjacent possibilities, rather than being ruled by her hormones. And although it sometimes seemed too much to change, she had increasing success in making this record shift.

Shirley would notice when her mood was getting dark. Then she would actually identify the minute of time, declaring what she wanted to experience, saying something like, 'It's 10:59 on April 4 and I am recording something this very moment. What do I want to record?' She would smile just at the thought of being able to make a difference.

Then she would think any one of a dozen thoughts that brought her happiness, and she affirmed that she had changed the record of that moment – and brought herself happiness, too. The more moments she did this, the greater the momentum of her joyous energy! Eventually a greater happiness took hold in her life, significantly liberating her from a difficult pattern that she thought she'd be stuck in for a long time.

After succeeding at making countless momentary changes in mood, she decided to work on her desired weight loss using the same approach. When eating her meals or bingeing on late-night snacks, she would stop and ask herself, 'What am I recording in this moment, in this choice?'

When she recognized the times that she was deepening her old records of addiction and unconscious behavior, she stopped and affirmed, 'Right now I choose to record strength, record change, and record the ability to let go.' This gave her the power to change the behavior then and there.

She would then take just a moment to visualize the change in her big record book – along with the statement, 'At this moment, Shirley happily made the choice to stop eating.' Each of these experiences inscribed new records in her life, and seeing them in her mind's eye made her feel empowered, more hopeful, and more in control than ever before.

There were times, however, when she forgot to intervene. If she realized too late, she would again visualize herself writing in her Life Record Book, this time saying that she forgave herself and knew she was capable of getting stronger and stronger. Even this new vision of placing self-love and self-forgiveness in her Eternal Records seemed to shift her feelings and bring a greater peace to her heart.

These two experiments were so successful that Shirley thought she would use the process to shift her whole relationship with food. She had been in the habit of eating for no reason, stuffing down a lot of food without being really aware of what the experience felt like. But she knew that wasn't healthy – or spiritually driven. So she added some other new approaches to create new patterns and to record a healthy attitude toward food.

She started when she woke up in the morning, taking a few minutes to think about the day ahead and recording a brief image of her mealtime activities. She saw herself eating slowly and consciously enjoying the experience. She then placed these images on the screen of her Present Records, often even putting a time and date stamp on the film as she saw it play out.

Then, as she went through the day and it came time to eat, she would stop for a few moments and think of the image she had recorded on her screen. She also took a moment to record a new intention in her Life Book, saying, 'I eat slowly and consciously, feeling the pleasure and appreciation of the food I am eating.'

She would then record the heart-felt desire to sit leisurely at her kitchen table and be more deliberate and aware. She enjoyed this new sensation, eating slowly instead of just stuffing everything down without any sense of presence in her body – or gratitude in her heart. She found she now had a different relationship with food, and a different sense of her own power – as well as the liberty to employ it.

It took a while, but Shirley eventually lost most of the weight she had gained. Her depression lifted, too, and whenever she found herself returning to old feelings and behaviors, she simply stopped to record a new moment of thought or behavior, posting it directly in her Personal Record Book. She always remembered her adjacent possibilities, knowing that if she created new records in her personal life now, it would lead to wonderful feelings of strength and a magnetic resonance that would fill her records with happiness in the future.

Exercise: Writing your records every present moment

Becoming conscious of your adjacent possibilities hugely accelerates your ability to take your power back – and redirect the Present and Future Records of your life. In fact, you can consciously and purposefully write the records of this moment and any moment you desire. You can also write about any activity you're engaged in, whether it's during this moment, or planned for an hour ahead or the day in front of you. All it takes is a few seconds, a clear intention, and keeping open to your options and your personal power. Here are the steps for writing the records of the present moment.

1. Take some time to identify your Present Record patterns. What are the thoughts, beliefs, and even words you'd like to shift to a more loving, honoring, empowered, or optimistic viewpoint? What are the emotional patterns you'd like to change? In other words, what are some of your patterns that you'd like to rewrite? Jot these things down in your Record Journal in order to prepare for the process of changing your Present Records.

2. Before you start the day, consider your potential opportunities for writing a new record. Each moment of self-actualized choice is another instance where you can change your records (and change your life.) So bring a deeper sense of your own power to this process, knowing that you can record at least a single moment of change.

3. Whenever possible, identify a moment of potential change and ask yourself, 'What do I want to record in this moment? What behavior, thought, or choice do I want to be placed in my Eternal Records right now?'

4. Breathe deeply and take a moment to visualize yourself engaging in that new choice. Also visualize yourself writing that choice in your Personal Record Book.

5. Then let yourself take the specific action that supports that choice in that moment. Whether it's changing a thought or engaging in a different behavior, see yourself doing it and then actually do it!

6. Affirm the emotion you're recording in this new choice; for example, 'Right now I'm recording strength, optimism, peace, honoring, dignity, grace, the ability to let go...' and so on.

7. Smile and take another moment to affirm appreciation for yourself and for the change that you've made. Know that every moment counts!

You can do this exercise in any instant of Record Creation, but you can also do it in anticipation of some particular time to come. For instance, when you take a few minutes at the beginning of the day to visualize your day ahead, especially consider the times or situations that may be challenging to you. This creates an awareness of the records you want to create in that situation – and a reminder that you have the power to change at any time. This is the ultimate empowerment. When you bring your consciousness to your life, your life will change!

Your Present Records are always evolving, always ready to be changed. They are a vital, living representation of the power and choices in your life. Whenever you notice an opportunity to record a new direction now, make the choice to redefine your moment. The lure of old habits may tempt you to repeat the unwanted stuff, but you can muster up the will, the courage, or just the self-discipline to seize the moment! Call upon the power of your spirit (see page 131) to help you make your change. However you do it, know that each and every Present Record change – even if just for a single moment – writes something new, something strong, something that will plant your Eternal Records with the seeds of value, purpose, and profound happiness.

SUMMARY

✦ The present is your best and *only* time to take action in any direction, whether it is spiritual, personal, or professional. By setting down a clear record that speaks your truth and reveals your highest intentions, you brighten your present life and enhance potential future consequences.

✦ Together with your thoughts, your emotions are the strongest components in both your record creation and the quality of your life.

✦ One of the highest intentions you can have is to make thought and behavioral choices that honor you. This action reaches through time to record health and happiness throughout your life.

✦ In any moment there are dozens of adjacent possibilities. Whenever you notice an opportunity to record a new direction, make the choice to redefine yourself and your moment now.

Chapter 8

The Realm of the Spirit

The world of spirit offers a very important connection to the Akashic Records. From your own spirit, your higher self, to the guides, masters, family and friends who have passed, the vibration of this higher energy resonates more easily with the frequency of the records. As a result, these entities can be messengers from the records themselves. You can even receive information from the angelic realm, so it's important to learn how to connect.

Angels and guides to the Akashic Records

All spirit – even your own – can easily resonate with the Akashic Field, but there are some energetic and heavenly beings that are more commonly connected with the Record experience. Metatron is considered one of the first angels. He's seen as the scribe, the record-keeper, a natural and powerful force in the *Akasha*. He is also a very ancient entity, often said to have predated Michael. In fact, many people call Metatron the first Michael.

Uriel is another angel who is closely connected to the Akashic Records. This angel of inspiration is also called the Fire of God. You may see Uriel as male or female. In fact, most angels can be seen in different genders. Since they are non-physical light beings, they use gender to reveal the kind of energy they bring.

In addition to these Akashic Record angels, you have a wonderful, ancient guide to the records, an angel or spiritual guide that reveals the fundamental truths that are important for your understanding. You may not see this guide all the time, but he or she will develop a relationship with you and be present for significant revelations. I call this person the 'Holder of the Truth,' the guardian of the profound spiritual truths that bring us understanding and growth.

I myself have had three experiences where a specific spirit, someone who seemed like a monk or holy man, brought me very important information for that time in my life. A recent one was in a dream where I was taught about the decoding and coding system that I wrote about in my book, *Your Quantum Breakthrough Code*. The same man also appeared to me in a powerful near-death experience. He led me to the river that I would have to pass over in order to get to the other side.

But my first exposure to this spirit was when I was just 16 or 17. He came to me in a dream and told me all about reincarnation, telling me that I would need to know such things one day. He also took me to different places in the energetic realm, showing me different light beings and explaining the things we do as spirits between our earthly existences. It's clear that this spirit has a deep connection with me, showing up at important times with important information. He may be with me more than I know, and I am always open to receiving more from him.

You have a special Truth Holder and other guides that carry life-changing inspiration from the Akashic Records – if you just open up to their presence. They have a personal interest in you, and you can forge close connections with them and with other spirit guides. Whenever you do the Sacred Temple meditation and other processes, you will be able to invite the angels, the Holder of the Truth, and other guides. You can ask them specific questions or request their assistance in any endeavor. They are always available, loving, interested, and always willing to help.

Angels and their expertise

There are countless angels and guides that you can turn to for information from the records, but we are going to be discussing the most commonly known ones here. Just as we human beings have areas of expertise, the angelic entities that are all around you each have their own specialty, too. Of course, any angel has access to the entirety of the Akashic Records, so each one can answer virtually any question for you – or bring you any information you may need. As a result, if you have one angel that you work with consistently, you can turn to that one as your Record Guide no matter what kind of information or energy you may need. This is true for your guardian angel, also a wonderful light being who has been there for you your whole life.

Remember, the Akashic Records hold energy as well as information, and just as the angels can bring very specific information and inspiration to you, they can also bring any specific type of energy that you desire. The records hold the vibrations of courage, strength, love, peace, and power, and the angels can bring these wonderful vibrations to you whenever you may need them.

The Eternal Records are filled with every act of courage, and that courage can touch your soul. The history of love in all its forms is available to you and can open your heart to the experience of loving yourself and others. In fact, this is a part of the Record's purpose: to hold the energies of all truth and power – and the angels can help to bring the exact resonance that you need at just the right time.

Keeping this in mind, it can be helpful to know the specific areas of each angel's expertise. Take a look at the following list to get acquainted with which angel tends to focus on the areas that you prioritize most. You can ask them to open the Akashic Records and bring you information about any problem that you may be trying to resolve. You can also ask them to bring the energetic vibrations of the action or emotion that they are most strongly connected with. Finally, you can also turn to the individual angels and guides to bring Akashic Inspiration, to help you hone your talents and skills, and to bring you amazing ideas for your creative projects. So as you go through the list, take note of the angels that resonate most with your own goals and needs. You can call on them by name or by purpose.

The list also reveals the most common colors that accompany each angel. This is helpful when doing the meditation at the end of the chapter, for you may see or sense a certain color and it could be indicative of that angel's presence, bringing the record information to you. You may see other colors, so use your own intuition to sense which angel you could be working with.

There is no right or wrong in this connection. Even if you don't see anything at all, your angels and guides are with you always. And since they are energetic beings of high intention and high vibration, they can offer a direct pipeline to all the power and information that the Akashic Records can present.

Michael, The Warrior

Michael is the angel of power, strength, initiative, and action. He brings information that can be helpful in situations where you are struggling over adversity, dealing with conflict, or just lacking courage. He can also help to bring you the energetic emotions of strength, conviction, greater responsibility, power, and determination where new action is needed. He is most often seen in colors of red.

Raphael, The Healer

Raphael can bring important assistance and information from the records when you are dealing with issues of the heart, whether it be about present relationships, releasing old patterns from difficult relationships, or even healing the pain of a broken heart. Raphael has a wonderful connection to the vibrations of pure love that resonate throughout the Eternal Records. You can call upon him for bringing the energies of physical healing, love, attracting relationships, and even ridding yourself of toxic patterns, difficult emotions, and old traumas.

Raphael has a strong focus on family and connecting children to parents. He can bring specific information when you are dealing with adoption, parenting choices, and any problems your children may have. He is often seen in different colors depending on the energy or information he brings. Greens and blues for travel and family connections, pinks and burgundies for love, and yellow, white, and gold or soft green for healing. All of the angels can bring great miracles, but Raphael is especially known for bringing miraculous healing energy and information.

I myself turned to Raphael when I was identifying and adopting my two children from Russia. There were countless occasions where I called upon him to assist us in the process, and every night I asked him to bring us the information that would connect us with just the right children. The synchronicity was amazing. The right agent, social worker, and orphanage each came into our experience in a mysterious and magical way. When obstacles appeared, I turned to Raphael and other spirits to help, and to bring us the information we would need to create the resolution we desired. The result he helped to create was a loving family with two wonderful children whom I know were destined to be with us.

Gabriel, The Messenger

Gabriel's expertise is communication of all kinds. If you are in a career that involves writing, journalism, public speaking, teaching, or counseling, Gabriel can open up the Akashic Records and provide great inspiration in all of these areas. Gabriel is especially helpful in bringing the energy of authenticity to your self-talk, so if you are in the habit of self-criticism or self-dismissal, you can call upon Gabriel to bring the energy of truth and the authenticity of your spiritual identity to your dealings with yourself.

The record of your soul truth is available to you, and it comes alive when you recognize your eternal value and power as the source of your true worth. Gabriel can help create a healthy ongoing dialogue with this, your true self, as opposed to the misinformation that you may have received from perhaps your parents or other authority figures. Remember, the Akashic Records hold all the wonderful details of your eternal power, value, and deserving. And Gabriel, who is usually seen in shades of blue, can open up those vibrant and life-changing memories for you.

Chamuel, Seeker of God

Chamuel can also bring powerful healing energy from the records. He is often seen as the angel of support, purpose, and assurance. He can bring specific information for healing, or to help you get back in balance whenever you're feeling fragmented, unfocused, or uncentered. Chamuel can also bring both the information and energy of purpose and direction. His colors are bright yellow for healing or a column of gold for centering.

Arael, Lion of God

Like Michael, Arael can help to bring the energies of courage and confidence. These Akashic energies and information can open you up to being more trusting or open, but they can also bring new ideas during creative projects. Arael can also bring you information about nature and animals, as well as energies of rejuvenation. Colors are orange for courage, gold for confidence, and white or pink for trust and intimate connections. You may also see a lion or animals of the woods when Arael is present.

Urial, The Fire of God

Urial is the angel of growth, transformation, inspiration, and intuition. Connecting with this angel can be an extremely powerful experience when you are trying to tap into the Akashic Records for inspiration regarding any kind of endeavor. From the artistic to the scientific, the pipeline of important data is always open through this angelic entity.

Urial can also open you up to the energy of intuition and connection, and the profound wisdom of spiritual truth. Urial's colors are the yellow-red of transformation, fire, and creativity, as well as white, indigo or violet for spirit connection.

Metatron, Keeper of the Archives

As we have seen, Metatron is considered one of the oldest and most powerful of all angels. He is also called 'The Link Between God and Man' or 'The Liberating Angel.' Since he is the record-keeper, he can tap into the Akashic Records for any reason, but especially to help find the wisdom of antiquity and the clarity of true thinking.

Metatron can also help to deliver the energies of peace of mind and unification with Divine Consciousness. He is extremely helpful when you are trying to realign your thoughts with your truth, as Gabriel is with your self-talk. His colors are usually indigo, white, or bright yellow like sunlight.

These are just a few of the angels that can help you tap into the unlimited information and vibration of your own Personal Records as well as the Records of Eternal Life. There are many more angels and spirits, and if you are accustomed to working with others, let yourself continue to deepen your relationships there. But it's also wise to open up to some new connections. And if you've never worked with the angels before, now is the time to start.

It is extraordinarily helpful to forge genuine relationships with these entities and work with them on a regular basis. It may seem strange at first to call upon an angel or guide to receive Akashic information, but consider their high vibration and Divine intention. They resonate at the highest levels with Universal synchronicity and with the records themselves. They also long to assist and help, and they have the power to spark an unending flow of amazing inspiration that can manifest in wonderful new experiences in every area of your life.

Spirit guides to the Akashic Records

Anyone in spirit can help you tap into the vast information that the Akashic Records hold, whether they be friends or family members that have passed on or Ascended Masters with very particular intentions. The reason it's so easy for spirit to gain access is that without the density of physical form, their vibration resonates more closely with the frequency of the records themselves.

Like the angels, your guides are always available to tap into the Akashic Records and bring information, inspiration, and solutions of all kinds. In fact, you can be guided by an unlimited number of loving souls. These are spiritual experts that can help you in any area that you desire. The different types of guides include:

Friends, family, business and personal connections from this life

The people in your life who have passed on (whether you knew them or not) often extend themselves to help and inspire you. A guide could be someone who loves you and wants to bring assistance, or it could be an expert who worked with you and who can continue to help you in that area now. It can also be a family member from a past generation who has an interest in you and your endeavors. And like a guardian angel, you have a personal guide who has been with you much of your life. This guide loves you deeply and has a personal interest in helping you achieve immeasurable happiness and success.

Talent or teacher guides

These are entities that may be known or unknown to you and are attracted to your goals and work by virtue of their own passions and interests in their lifetimes. They may just appear at appropriate times or when required for guidance in a specific project. For example, Mozart may bring inspiration for composing, Shakespeare for writing, Degas for painting, Julia Child for cooking. This is especially likely when you have some sort of fondness for, or connection to, the expert or their work. In addition, people who have actually been your teachers in this and other lives could be working hard in the energetic realm to bring you the inspiration and information you are looking for. Be open to their loving presence. There is a meditation in Chapter 11 (*see page 214*) that will help to forge these connections.

Past-life guides

These spirit beings have actually shared past lives with you and spark a renewed connection to a personal purpose from the past. They not only help to inform you of your own past-life experiences, they can also help in the specific areas or relationships that they experienced with you. For example: a husband from a past life may work on finding you a husband now; a past boss in spirit may bring information that can help you find a job.

Ascended Masters

Ascended Masters are very high-energy entities who have walked the Earth and had a physical life but have now chosen to work with humanity from the energetic realm. Like the angels, they often have specific purposes – or energies – that they like to focus on. Ascended Masters can be guides and healers, opening the Eternal Records and offering advice, wisdom, and solutions on everything from the personal to the global level.

Some of the most commonly witnessed and profoundly helpful Ascended Masters are:

Jesus Christ

Jesus walked the earth to bring great changes to history and humanity itself. Whether your religious belief holds him to be God or a prophet or simply a master, he has limitless power to help and heal. He is master of many things, including Divine Master of Love and Spiritual Wisdom; Teacher of tolerance and compassion; World Consciousness shifter and miraculous Healer. Jesus brings the Akashic energy and information of healing, deeper wisdom, compassion, understanding, and Divine Experience and Expression. He is available to you at all times and for all reasons, but his focus is pure love. His colors are yellow for healing, pink or green for love, white for Divinity and clarity. Symbols that indicate the presence of Jesus are fish, a lamb, or a cross.

The Buddha

There are several historical and legendary figures called the Buddha, including Gautama Buddha, Siddhartha, and Shakyamuni Buddha. Born approximately 563BCE, he relinquished a privileged life to look for the answers to religious and philosophical questions. His teachings filled the *Akasha* with important information and promoted enlightenment through detachment and meditation. Connect with him to enhance your energies of reflection, transcendence, release of attachment, and to find inner peace in your life. His colors are usually gold, orange, and red.

Elijah (Elias)

This master has a history in many cultures and religions, including Greek, Hebrew, and Christian. A prophet from around 900BCE, he was said to have raised the dead, brought fire down from the sky, and been lifted up by a whirlwind.

According to the Gospel of Matthew, John the Baptist is thought to be the reincarnation of Elias, and he, too, is also considered to be an Ascended Master. Both identities bring Akashic guidance and inspiration. They can also infuse your life with truly dynamic energy when strength is needed in situations of conflict. They also bring assistance with personal power, healing, and devotion. The colors and sensations of fire, wind, and water are often associated with him.

Imhotep, Egyptian High Priest and Architect

Imhotep's name means 'the one that comes in peace.' He built Egypt's first pyramid, but he was also a poet, doctor, astrologer, and sage. Imhotep is said to bring Akashic wisdom concerning medicine and healing, as well as inspiration regarding architecture, design, poetic expression, and even prediction. A common symbol for him is a pyramid, and colors are the yellows of the sun and sand.

Saint-Germain

Also known as Master Rakozy, this Hungarian alchemist, painter, composer, and scientist lived in the 1700s. He is the master of ceremony and ritual, discipline, groups and organizations, and he can open the Records for these reasons, as well as for creativity and shifting consciousness. He is especially helpful with group guidance and shared consciousness, and he is said to be working on a global scale. His color is purple and his image is the world or globe.

Hilarion

This master is also called 'the Healer and Bringer of Truth.' He lived in 290ce, and there are those that also consider him to be Saul of Tarsus, master of healing and clear understanding; he is also the master of intellect, science, detail, and follow-through. He brings Akashic Record wisdom for physical or mental healing, clarity and truth, as well as energy when a miracle is needed. His colors are earth tones, yellows and golds, and some see him holding a lantern.

Teresa of Avila

This master of devotion, healing, and self-discipline was a Medieval Carmelite nun who lived in austerity and prayer. She wrote *The Way of Perfection* and *The Interior Castle*. Connect with her for Akashic Inspiration and for a closer relationship with God, deeper devotion, and stronger self-discipline – or for personal or physical healing. Her colors are reds, pinks, and earth tones.

Exercise: Steps for spirit and angel communication

The following process is designed to help you connect with the wonderful entities in spirit. It may seem easy but it is also very effective, and the more you practice it, the more you will forge ever-deepening relationships that will support you throughout your life.

1. Breathe deeply and relax. Quiet your mind and let go of any concerns.

2. Release analysis and expectation. Don't think about what you want to happen; just allow the information to come.

3. Take a few more deep breaths and drop your consciousness into your heart. At this point you can invite a loving spirit by name or by purpose.

4. Take a moment to sense, feel, or see if there are any colors present with this angel or guide.

5. Notice if you get any images that may represent a specific angel, such as a horn with Gabriel, a sword with Michael, a book or scroll with Uriel or Metatron, an animal with Arael, etc. (A guide may have an identifying image as well, such as a piano for Mozart or quill pen for Shakespeare.)

6. Open your heart and mind to receiving any information that spirit may give you – in any way that is most comfortable. You may receive information about who the angel, guide, or spirit is, as well as the information you are seeking.

7. As you get comfortable with the loving presence, you can ask a specific question or invite spirit to give you any information that you may need.

8. Allow yourself to receive the information as it is given. It may be in a word, a phrase, or an image. You may intuitively know the meaning right away, or you may have to wait as the meaning becomes clearer in the time to come.

9. Take a moment to ask if there is any more information the spirit wants to impart – for you personally or about any issue.

10. Thank the angel or guide for their love and assistance. Affirm your love, constant connection, and deep appreciation, and let this entity know that you are willing to receive spontaneous guidance at any time.

The spirit of your higher self

The spirit of your soul is one of the most powerful connections you can have to the Akashic Records. This eternal part of you is often called your 'higher self.' It's not *higher* because it's somehow better than your physical self, or because it's floating above you somewhere. It's called your higher self because it vibrates at a higher frequency than your personal and physical self. As such, it has a stronger resonant connection to Divine Consciousness and to all of the information, power, and resources of the energetic realm, including the vast expanse of the Akashic Field.

Your higher self actually knows more about what you need than you do, and it can provide all the solutions you seek. Because it has access to all the great fields of information and energy in the eternal realm it's important not to get so caught up in your physical and personal world that you dismiss this very powerful part of yourself.

It's also important to know that the expansiveness of your soul is not limited by the physical and mental restrictions of your personal self in this life. Your soul pre-existed this earthly experience and will continue to exist long after it. When you allow yourself to get out of your own way and release doubt and worry, you can align this eternal part of you with the resonance of the spirit of the Universe. When that happens, you can be truly inspired, receiving all sorts of Akashic energy and information, even at the most unexpected of times.

This synchronicity with Divine Mind and unlimited potential has been the source of amazing inventions and discoveries, and even wonderfully creative works in art, literature, and music. Take some time to meditate and get in touch with your higher self, your own eternal identity.

When you make the connection with this creative consciousness, you will gain access to the great fields of inspiration and the eternal wisdom of all ages – past, present, and future.

Opening the records through your intuition

People get intuitive hits all the time. Sometimes they listen; sometimes they don't. It's a high intention to develop a real comfort and readiness to use your intuition. This is one of the primary ways that you can personally tap the synchronicity of the Universe and the great field of consciousness that is the Akashic Records.

The kind of intuitive messages you receive may be mundane – like whether to carry an umbrella on a potentially rainy day. But it's just as likely you will receive valuable and extremely important information.

> *Your intuitive mind taps the Akashic Records regarding all your life issues – from simple helpful hints to life-changing projects.*

Here are some practical steps that will help to enhance the power of your intuition in your everyday life:

✦ Relax or meditate on a regular basis. In order to listen for Universal answers, it is important to quiet your mind and open yourself to receiving. Even just taking a few deep breaths and releasing your thoughts periodically will help to open this pipeline for you.

✦ Learn to listen to your gut feeling more often. In time you will be able to distinguish the voice of your intuition from the other voices in your head. Yet there are times when you may have to go deep within and listen to your heart to notice the difference.

✦ As often as possible, let your consciousness drift into a peaceful place in your heart center. The mental striving of life – along with having endless tasks and activities – can stop the flow of information. So let yourself stretch out, relax your muscles and your mind, and let your consciousness move into your heart center. This will help you to connect with the peaceful current of Universal love and guidance that is always available to you.

✦ Whenever you have a specific issue you're working on – or anything that you may need some guidance or inspiration about – let yourself request this from your own eternal spirit. Keep a notebook by your bed, and when you go to bed at night, jot down the question, the concern, or the issue that you're thinking about along with a simple intention: *'I open myself to spirit's assistance. I am receiving helpful information in a way that I can remember and understand.'*

✦ As you fall asleep, direct your higher self to open up to the Akashic Records. Whatever information you may get, make sure you jot it down. Even your dreams may have important answers for you, so remain open to seeing the truth. If you get some information in your dreams, jot it down, even if it doesn't seem to make sense at first. You will be receiving more energy, clarity, and information as time goes on.

✦ Trust what you get. Whether at night or as you're moving through your day, your soul and other spirits are bringing you Akashic guidance. Let yourself hone your intuitive skills and believe in your eternal self. Bring this attitude and intention to receive into everything you do. You will be surprised at what comes your way!

✦ The energy of your spirit is always a part of both your present and eternal self. Your soul is a force in the world even now, and your essence has the power to tap into the great field where all wisdom, inspiration, and guidance is stored. As a radiantly vibrating eternal spirit, you have the power to connect with the world of spirit and with the unending power of the Divine, your ultimate source of all-embracing love and assistance!

The Divine connection

There is one more spiritual force that can easily open the door to the Akashic Records for you. Whether you call this creative source *God*, the *Divine*, or the *Universe*, this beautiful presence of higher consciousness is also an ever-present source of meaningful solutions. This Divine source of creation vibrates in every wave and particle of the cosmos. As a result, it spans the breadth and width of the unending Akashic Records – and everything that carries the Records also carries the Divine within it. When you forge a powerful connection with this dynamic field of consciousness and creation, you will receive valuable guidance along with surprising assistance in future manifestation.

It's important to see yourself as an expression of this Divine energy in life, for it embodies the inherent value of your humanity along with the profound reality of your eternal truth. There is such a deep sense of peace and constancy that comes from the recognition of the Divine within you. It starts with the recognition that you are spirit first. You don't need to do or be anything different to be special. Your sacred identity is the real source of your value and worthiness in this life. So it's time to acknowledge this truth and let go of the conditional self-acceptance that consistently rejects the beautiful holiness of yourself.

The vital presence of the Divine within is *always* your ultimate source of worthiness. When you understand this truth and embrace this wonderful realization, your heart will open to the unlimited assistance and blessings that the Universe has to offer. This is the most receptive vibration of all. Sensing the Divine within awakens you to your Akashic Truth, and it opens every door to a beautiful life and brilliant happiness!

SUMMARY

◆ You have a special Truth Holder and many other guides that carry life-changing inspiration from the Akashic Records.

◆ You can develop meaningful relationships with countless angels and guides, and you can always turn to them for support and record information.

◆ There are a number of practical steps that can enhance your power of intuition, including relaxing, asking, and trusting what you get.

◆ The creative source of the Universe is a driving force in your life and in the world, and you can call upon this power at any time.

Chapter 9
Wisdom of the World

The information in the Akashic Records is not limited to your personal history or even the shared history of the cultures and countries throughout time. In addition to that vast amount of data, you can also use the Records to inform yourself about very real truths regarding the physical and natural worlds – here on Earth and even in other places.

Many people seem to think that there are special places, some called the Hall of Learning, Education, or Inspiration, which are specifically dedicated to the type of information that people need for invention or discovery. They often imply that these types of records are more difficult to access, but nothing could be further from the truth.

The reality is, like all of the information and energy in the records, the entirety of the wisdom of the world, in all its forms and applications, vibrates in even the subtlest resonance, as well as the strongest wave frequencies of existence. It is available to any of us at any time, and the best way to tap this kind of information is to align our own intentions with the resonant waves of the information itself. When we do this, the information we are looking for matches our own personal vibration in an interesting process known as entrainment.

Entraining to the Akashic Field

Entrainment is a type of energetic synchronicity that can bring about amazing and often unexpected consequences. It starts when energetic vibrations come together, and when their rhythm or frequencies have matching qualities, they tend to fall into a synchronicity with each other. When we are in alignment with our purpose, it creates a fluid connection with the records that causes the information to flow at just the right time and in just the right way – often without any conscious direction at all.

The following case study shows how the records can work in this way.

Easy as pie

Sarah was a phenomenal baker. She made delicious pies, pastries, and cakes, and she thoroughly enjoyed the process of baking as well as the results she came up with.

When Sarah heard about a contest for the best original pie, she became determined to create the best pie possible. She continued baking and practicing new recipes, which were all delicious, but not quite having the ultimate effect she was looking for. She wasn't desperate, but she continued experimenting and honing the recipe she had been focusing on.

One day, when driving home from work at her bake shop, she was stopped at a red light, listening to her favorite music and not thinking about anything in particular. Gazing off into the distance, all of a sudden the missing element of the recipe she had been working on came to her. First she saw the ingredient she needed to add then she clearly saw how and when she should add it to the recipe.

She seemed to know immediately that this was the solution she had been looking for, but she went directly home and tried the new recipe exactly as it had been revealed to her in those moments of inspiration. She loved the results, and so did the judges of the original pie contest held in her town. She won first place.

It's important to know that this is an ongoing function of the Akashic Records. In spite of all the baking and cooking that has been done all over the world and throughout time, there are thousands, or even hundreds of thousands, of wonderful yet presently unknown recipes of all kinds. All of that information is vibrating now in the Realm of the Records, waiting to be revealed.

In fact, if your energy is aligned – like Sarah's – to a specific intention, it's entirely possible that the information you seek will come unbidden, and at the seemingly most unlikely times. This is the synchronicity that comes from entraining with the Akashic Field, and examples of this incredible process of spontaneously gaining record information can be seen in some of the most profound scientific discoveries in history.

Written in nature

Unlimited information and boundless creativity fill every corner of the cosmos. Our resonant connection with the Universal flow makes every bit of wisdom and inspiration available to us at any time. It is only our own disbelief and agitating distractions that stop us from being in the flow. Once we open up and get out of our own way, however, amazing things can happen in the most mystical of ways.

This is the type of incredible experience that happened to Kary Mullis, a California chemist who had been dedicating his work to understanding and decoding DNA. In his book, *Dancing Naked in the Mind Field*, Mullis describes how he had been unceasingly working in the lab, trying to find a solution to DNA identification. After devoting countless hours to this endeavor, he felt he needed a break.

So he decided to engage in his favorite hobby, surfing, and to go to his cabin in Anderson Valley, California. He let go of his scientific quest, and he was looking forward to his weekend off. What he didn't realize, however, was that he was going to be working more that weekend than he had in recent memory. A stunning revelation from the records was on its way.

He had been enjoying the view as he was driving through the California valley, gazing up at the hills and at the beautiful blossoms on the trees. As he was taking in the stunning scenery, the solution he had been seeking suddenly appeared to him, almost as if it were written in the trees and the hills! He was stunned and surprised, but he pulled over to write out what he saw. Upon looking at the theory he had written down, he realized that in that sparkling moment of inspiration, he had invented the polymerase chain reaction (PCR), a hugely important breakthrough regarding the many revelations that DNA can provide.

Mullis called his colleagues and they all got together over the weekend, working through the information. He continued to test it in the lab, but the original solution proved to be correct. In fact, he now wondered why he hadn't come upon it earlier, since the answer seemed so simple. Interestingly enough, that simple yet vital piece of information had been stored in the Akashic Records, waiting for his matching resonance to receive it.

This revelation brought Mullis the Nobel Prize, and the importance of its truth is seen throughout the world. The resulting process from his discovery has widely expanded the understanding and uses of DNA, radically changing forensic criminology, as well as predicting and saving people from genetically predisposed diseases.

But this profoundly influential discovery is not an isolated event. Countless discoveries, inventions, and even great works of music, literature, and art have been sourced in synchronistic connections between individuals and the Akashic Field, the unlimited consciousness of information and creation. In fact, the magic of spontaneous inspiration has even surfaced as seemingly 'accidental' events.

Unexpected gifts from the records

Revelations from the records can come in a number of ways. Sometimes they are spontaneously inspired, sometimes they are purposefully sought after and eventually found, and sometimes the information imposes itself (perhaps with the help of spirit) upon the investigator through an unplanned occurrence that may seem like an accident. Such was the case for bacteriologist Alexander Fleming in 1928 when an accidental discovery in a contaminated Petri dish would go on to help save millions of lives.

Fleming had returned to his laboratory after being on vacation, finding a number of used Petri dishes that he had set aside in order to clear his workbench. He had been working to find a chemical that would kill bacteria without doing harm to the human body. While checking out the various dishes – simply to see which could be reused – he found that one had grown a mold in it, and that mold had actually killed the Staphylococcus aureus bacteria that had been growing in the dish.

The mold turned out to be Penicillium, and Fleming named the first antibacterial agent Penicillin. Although Fleming discovered Penicillin in this purely accidental manner, it took two other scientists and several years for it to be refined into the usable medication that it eventually became. In time, it became the wonder drug of World War II, saving countless people from infected wounds, diphtheria, gangrene, tuberculosis, and pneumonia. In 1945 all three scientists received the Nobel Prize, yet it was Fleming's accidental record inspiration that started it all.

Charles Goodyear made another accidental but history-changing discovery when he was searching for a way to vulcanize rubber, allowing it to maintain its elasticity. Goodyear had worked tenaciously on this project, eventually putting his family in debt, but he would never give up. Goodyear had originally thought that heat was a part of the problem he was solving. However, when he accidently left a batch of rubber on a stove one day, he discovered that heat was actually the solution.

He realized that if you remove sulfur from rubber before heating it, it would retain its elasticity. In 1844, Charles Goodyear was given the patent for vulcanized rubber. Years later, when automobiles became the rage, two men from Ohio named their tire company after the man who accidentally learned how to tame rubber.

Wilson Greatbatch invented the pacemaker while he was actually working on a heart-rhythm recorder. In the process he added an electrical component causing the device to produce electrical pulses rather than simply recording them. He immediately realized that he had inadvertently found a way to stimulate a heartbeat electrically. He spent the next few years miniaturizing the device and was granted a patent for the implantable pacemaker in 1962. Like Fleming, his accidental inspiration has gone on to save countless lives all over the world.

These are compelling stories, but what do they have to do with Sarah's recipe, the decoding of DNA, and the Akashic Records? The fact is, there are some important unifying elements to all of these situations, and they revolve around *energy*. If you want to open yourself to the records' spontaneous inspiration or accidental discovery, you will have to become more conscious of your own energy. When the right energetic elements come together, your life force can reach out into the world and extract from the Akashic Records the exact inspiration that you need most.

Alignment of intention, action, and letting go

Whether it's a simple recipe for a tasty pie or one of the most important biological breakthroughs of the century, the Akashic Records offer an unlimited store of information that can benefit mankind in any number of ways. But how do such inspirations and even seemingly 'accidental' discoveries take place? Well, there is a recipe that can help *you* cook up one of these amazing experiences in your life as well.

The first two ingredients are *intention* and *action*. These are energetic elements that drive your life force resonance in the direction of potentially powerful connections of all kinds, including the Akashic Records. But the synchronicity that generates this kind of magic calls for very specific types of action and intention. Let's examine how all these elements come together to open the flow of record information and create incredible miracles.

1. Intention

We engage in countless intentions throughout the day. Many are actually driven by the simple functions of everyday life. For example, we intend to drive to work, eat lunch, call friends, get some housework done. These activities all carry intentions, but we rarely perceive them that way.

Most people consider intentions only to be related to goals like making money, finding love, or getting a new job. And although these are all valid goals, they don't always represent the highest intentions that really drive the information results.

The types of personal intention that truly create magical outcomes include the following energies:

✦ The purpose of creating something valuable – or pleasing – in a heart-centered sort of way.

✦ A genuine desire to serve, inform, assist, or enhance the lives of others.

✦ An alignment with one's own life purpose, interests, and daily activities.

You can see how these elements of intention came together in the cases of Sarah's pie and Mullis decoding DNA. Though they are vastly different, they each represent a purpose of value, a genuine desire to enhance the life experience, and a personal alignment with their interests and activities. It would be very unlikely for Mullis to come up with an incredible pie recipe – and nearly impossible for Sarah to decode DNA. These discoveries simply did not resonate with their intentions or their actions, which is the second ingredient in receiving magical information from the records.

2. Action

In these and in all of the 'accidental' discoveries mentioned above, there is the common thread of repeated (and intentional) action. When a person dedicates much of their time and energy to a certain kind of pursuit then that repeated effort opens the door to receiving more record information, which can promote their endeavors in significant ways. Your daily action creates an energetic momentum in your life, and that energy can either block or accelerate the record inspiration that can come your way.

Here's the type of action that can ignite your reception:

- ✦ Aligning your tasks with the higher intentions described above.

- ✦ Repeated activities that become a part of your passion or your lifestyle.

- ✦ Focused (but not desperate) action in the pursuit of a specific goal.

In all of the cases cited above, the activities of the individuals were aligned with their higher intentions to bring something valuable to the world. They had a genuine passion for their goals, and they focused their daily action on them.

3. Letting Go

In these cases – and in so many more – the final piece of the magical information puzzle is the act of letting go. This is not only true for tapping into the Akashic Records, it's also true for so many other pursuits. The joy of surrender, the release of striving and urgency, the peace of trusting, all of these are powerful energies that accelerate synchronicity and manifestation.

Mullis didn't find his answer in the lab. It came unbidden as he was blissfully viewing the wonders of nature around him on his drive. His action and intention had already been set in that direction, and he was relaxed and unwittingly open to receiving. It was the alignment of his genuine desire and his present peace of mind that moved the information from the Akashic Field into his reality.

Again, he is not alone. Einstein often said that his most important discoveries came at a time when he wasn't thinking about the problem at hand. Thomas Edison was frequently reported to get the answers he was looking for when he awoke from a nap on the cot he kept in his laboratory.

This is the beauty of the Akashic Records. The information is waiting for you in great vibrating fields of consciousness, ready to spin out and inspire you, if you let yourself relax, open up and receive. So create an intention to bring something valuable to your life and to the lives of others. Whether it's a new recipe, a musical composition, or a great scientific discovery, let yourself feel passionate about your goal and take regular and focused action in that direction. Then take a break. Let go, get away, trust, and be peaceful. That's when the magic happens.

Expanding information – more from morphogenetic fields

As we discussed in Chapter 2 (*see page 35*), the morphogenetic fields of consciousness and information are always vibrating, expanding with accumulating interests and intentions of like resonance. The morphic resonance of discovery and invention can inspire people in all sorts of ways, for clearly the fields don't merely receive information, they send it out as well.

There is information that is even now expanding and reaching out, an ongoing function of the consciousness field that we call the Akashic Records – one that is filled with both future discovery and present inspiration. These patterns of expansion and acceleration are waiting and accumulating in the great field of the consciousness of mankind, responding to those who align their intention and their action – and who are truly open to receiving.

In fact, the information of discovery is there for all to receive, and sometimes more than one person at or near the same time taps the same information. This is a function of energy expansion, which moves the world to greater readiness. The readiness of the individuals involved – and the readiness of the world – aligns with the information itself, expanding discovery across the planet. This explains the phenomenon that can be seen throughout recent history, simultaneous invention: the process where different parties discover the same information in unplanned ways, often unknown to each other.

Simultaneous invention – shared information

Medical discovery, technological invention, and scientific breakthroughs have often happened in far-off places yet at the same time with the same results. Here are just a few examples of how information from the Akashic Field can reach different people at the same time, resulting in significant advancement, and in some cases considerable competition.

The light bulb

Though many people believe that Thomas Edison invented the light bulb, several others had been working on the same project and had actually beaten him to the punch. What Edison really discovered was a more efficient filament in producing light. And for a while his product ruled the market.

The telephone

Alexander Graham Bell is credited with inventing the telephone, yet others in the U.S. and elsewhere were devising the same or similar systems. In fact, another inventor applied for a patent for the telephone the same day as Bell, but he lost his claim in a heated court battle.

The automobile

Dozens of people throughout Europe and the U.S. were inspired to create different forms of this invention. In this, as in the other cases, the information field of auto technology was expanding rapidly due to the timing and readiness of the planet connecting with so many people putting their energy and intentions forward. That field of information expanded, and then reached out to inspire people in various countries across the world. Although many Americans think that Henry Ford invented the automobile, there are others in Germany, France, and the U.S. who actually claim that title. Ford went on to develop and perfect the assembly line, however, and his was one of the first companies in the world to produce affordable cars for the masses.

The television

Philo T. Farnsworth was known as the inventor of the television. In fact, it was called the Farnsworth Invention before the word 'television' was coined. But really, several scientists – both individually and in teams – came up with the important features of radio imagery before Farnsworth did. So many people were involved in this process of invention at this time, it's impossible to say who really was the first to invent the apparatus that billions of people now use every single day.

The hologram of your records in the Universe

This is all fascinating information, and it certainly bears witness to the presence of an expansive field of vital and vibrant information. This energy and consciousness can move us forward, whether in our individual lives or in our global experience. But as interesting as all this technological advancement and medical discovery is, what exactly does it mean to you?

It means that you are a part of an incredible tapestry of boundless information and vibrating cause and effect. The energy of the world moves to you, through you and all around you. The solutions you seek are closer than you think, though they may come in whispers and diaphanous shadows.

Your signature resonance is an accumulation
of every energetic part of you.

The resonance of your whole identity moves out in all directions and connects with Universal potential in a myriad of ways. This process of connection is a significant part of the Record Vibration of the World.

In fact, your resonance – and your records – connect with everyone else's to some degree or another. The people and solutions that resonate with you most will be drawn to you long before you consciously connect. This is what happened to many of the scientists and inventors in this chapter; their energy first connected with the Field of Solutions, and the answers came to them in real time. There are many solutions and supportive people that are responding to your present energy and intentions, and they can be drawn to your life in just the right time and place.

You are a very special, unique individual, and no one has the same signature records as you do – no one! As we discussed earlier, your Personal Records represent every part of you – past, present, and future potential. They vibrate with your emotions, beliefs, hopes, and fears; and those records expand with the fullness of the hologram that is your whole and eternal self.

A part of that self is the power of your soul, and it can connect with others on the soul level. This strong spirit identity is just as much a part of you as your personal self that may sometimes have nagging doubts or weakness. Yet in spite of its power, this amazing part of you can seem further away, and often its fullness doesn't feel as compelling as your physical sensations.

But this part of you is always there, always accessible, always willing to help. And, because it carries the records of your spiritual truth and eternal value and power, it can usually be of more help than most other things you turn to. In fact, the records of your soul-self carry all the grace, strength, wisdom, and understanding you will ever need. These records, with their grand memories, are available to help you now – and can accelerate your connections – at any time.

If you're unsure about your options, if you need strength when you're feeling powerless, trust when you're worried, or courage when facing conflict, your higher self can bring that to you. This holographic spiritual identity has experienced all of these qualities and remembers what they feel like. Not only that, your soul-self is connected to the power of the Universe, and all of the wisdom and infinite potential that it holds.

This wildly vibrant, magnetic part of yourself has the records of your truth written deep within, and you can call upon those wonderful vibrations any time you need. Not only can you call upon any quality you desire, you can send this wonderful part of yourself, with its records of beauty, deserving, and magnetism, out into the Universe to connect with the supportive people and beneficial situations that you long to bring into your life.

The Higher Self Holographic Projection process described below will help you with both of these intentions by

1. Calling upon the most powerful qualities your eternal records hold;

2. Sending out the hologram of your higher self, your most magnetic records, to connect with the solutions you seek in the Akashic Realm, bringing them to you in real time.

You can use the process to do one or the other – or even both. For example, if you're in a situation where you just need a quality that seems distant yet lives in your spiritual records, all you have to do is name it and feel the light of your soul bringing it to your heart, where it grows and becomes stronger.

Whether it's self-acceptance, peace, power, confidence, or anything else that you long to manifest from within, it's there vibrating within your Spiritual Records, ready to rise up and shine from the light of your eternal soul. You can experience this any time you choose, and the more you do this Higher Self Holographic Projection, the easier and more spontaneous it will become.

Exercise: Higher-self holographic projection

Your higher self has access to all of the wisdom and all of the experience you will ever need. In addition to the Akashic Records, it has access to all of the people in your life now and to all of the situations that you may experience in the future. By getting in touch with this part of you, you will be able to experience greater confidence, purpose and happiness, as well as attracting a happy and successful future. So use this time to tap into the strongest, most magnetic and most connective part of your nature.

Every time you do this process you will be stimulating the mystical forces of the Universe, not only connecting with the creative flow of abundance, but also with the Akashic Records, the unlimited field of information and inspiration that can help you in every area of your life. So let go of any outside thoughts or concerns and allow your body to relax and your mind to be quiet, as you open yourself to the powers of your higher self and to the unknown forces that are willing to assist you even now. This is a very important process, so it may be helpful to record it and use the process when you have about 15 minutes to relax. You are certainly worth it!

1. You are now going to count backward from three to one and with each descending number you will feel yourself going into a deeper and deeper relaxation. Three... Breathe deeply and feel a warm wave of relaxation moving throughout your body all the

way down your arms, all the way through your legs, down to your feet and toes. Two... You feel the sweet, heavy sense of relaxation as you let your consciousness drift easily and gently into your heart center now. One... Just allow yourself to continue to remain peaceful and relaxed.

2. Slowly you begin to notice a tiny bubble of light in the center of your being, shining gently near your heart center. Like an inflating balloon, you notice that light getting bigger and brighter with each gentle breath, until it fills your chest, sending out beautiful rays of light through your entire body.

3. Slowly you see or sense the globe of light starting to rise, gently lifting up and out of you until it is just above and in front of you, shining beautifully, softly, radiantly. You notice a beautiful energy emanating from an image in this light. It is a three-dimensional light image, a holographic image of your own higher self, your own powerful, eternal soul.

4. Take a moment now to look up at this energetic light image of your highest, most powerful self. Allow the sphere to turn so that you can see all sides of this radiant, beautiful, and powerful light image of yourself.

5. Picture the beautiful details of your eternal self clearly – smiling, beaming, shining brightly. Feel the energy of your higher self – peaceful yet powerful, capable of making great changes in your life.

6. First you feel the energy of personal power and confidence. It's a strong sense of courage pulsating in every direction out of this glowing part of yourself. Feel the energy of confidence, power, self-worth, and determination that is emanating to you and through you, filling you up with this personal power.

7. And now you notice that your higher self is projecting the energy of love and self-acceptance. You begin to feel a truly powerful love, the greatest love that the Universe can provide: the unending love of the Divine. And even if you feel you have never been loved before, your higher self, your soul, knows and has felt the unconditional, all-consuming love of the Divine.

8. Take a moment to feel this love flowing through you. You now know that you deserve to be loved and deserve to love yourself, and you choose to do so.

9. And now as you look up at this brilliant light of your true self, you feel a strength and belief in yourself like you've never felt before – a genuine high regard for yourself and confidence in your worth, and you know that you deserve a wonderful life.

10. Take a moment now to see and feel all of these brilliant energies in the hologram of your higher self. The confidence, the power, the love, the strength, the respect and belief in yourself – all emanating from within your eternal life source, your own eternal spirit. These qualities are always within you, always a part of who you really are.

11. Knowing that your higher self is projecting its most magnetic and resonant energy, you can now release it into the energetic realm, the great Akashic Field where all solutions lie. Now let yourself send this brilliant light of your higher self – with its radiant power and value – out into the Universe, allowing it to spread its energies outward in all directions. Your magnetic energies are radiating strongly outward into space and time, shining brightly in the distance for all to see and for the Universe to embrace.

12. You feel that something wonderful is about to happen, and you notice that there are many other lights off on the horizon, beginning to move toward the light of your own higher self in the distance.

13. You realize these lights are the manifestation of your deepest desires, the fulfillment of your dreams and goals, the solutions that you seek and the inspiration that you desire. Whether the connection has to do with a career goal, personal health, a creative project, or financial success – whatever it is, it's waiting for you in the energetic realm, in the Akashic Field of every potential, connecting with your own life force now.

14. The solutions you seek are on the horizon, energetically uniting with your own higher self. And as you look at the lights of these people, ideas, and solutions, you feel a strong attraction there. You know that the Universe is responding to your own eternal energy, your own brilliant light.

15. Knowing this, you can now bless and send the other light images back into the Universe, comfortable in the certainty that these wonderful solutions and outcomes are coming to you in space and time. Coming in response to your eternal energy.

16. Release all of the light images back into the Universe, and see your own holographic light returning to you. You know that this wonderful eternal self is always with you, always connected to the Akashic Field, willing to answer any questions and bring any strength or emotion that you desire.

17. The wonderful vibrations of your own light return to you now. So pull down this hologram of your highest, strongest, most resonant self – until it is all around you and you fill it like a glove.

18. You can feel its energies and powers filling you up, pulsating vibrantly within you, and radiating outward from you.

19. Your higher self is all around you now, all within you, always radiating from you. Feel the all-encompassing energy of strength, confidence, power, belief, love, and self-respect that it brings. Any

time that you need any of these energies or emotions – or any higher emotion that you desire – you know that you can call upon this wonderful hologram of your eternal self to bring it to you.

20. You are now going to count upward from one to three, slowly coming back to this time and space, filled with the wonderful sensations that your powerful eternal self has brought to you. One... Coming back to this time and space. Your eternal identity is always there to assist you, bringing information, energy, inspiration, and successful experiences into your life. Two... Back to this time and space now. In the time to come you will continue to make deeper connections with this powerful self that is with you always. Whatever you need, whether it's courage, assertiveness, peace, wisdom, patience, or power, simply take a deep breath, name the energy, and feel it pulsating within you and radiating outward from you. Your higher self is capable of giving you all that you need. Three... Back to this time and space now. The solutions you seek are already taking shape in the Akashic Field. Knowing this, you can completely let go and trust that you are open to receiving wonderful inspiration and support in magical and unexpected ways.

Romance in the Akashic Realm

I first came up with this Holographic Projection Meditation when I was going through my second divorce. (Let me amend that, for I am becoming more convinced that it isn't I who comes up with much of anything. I'm just a reporter on assignment in the Akashic Realm. Someone or something streams the information to me, and I try to get it out there.)

As I was saying, I was going through my second divorce, and although I never wanted to marry again, I knew I would be dating, and I wanted to be with someone responsible, sane, and compassionate. As I was falling asleep one night, it occurred to me that if I sent out my highest vibrations, I would then attract someone who would resonate with me at that level.

So I decided to send out the hologram of my higher self, vibrating with its most healthy and resonant frequencies. I visualized it projecting in time and space, and I affirmed that I was attracting my ideal partner. I started using this process in April, and by July I had met my present husband. (He talked me into it.) I was so impressed with the results that I put the meditation on a CD, and I've heard from countless people that they too have met their ideal love using the technique.

This showed me that the Akashic Records are filled with vital and vibrating connections. I supported this holographic intention by making honoring thoughts and choices in my daily life, and I knew I would find the right partner for me. I also used this Holographic Projection to find my wonderful publisher, Hay House, and, as I mentioned earlier, to identify my two adopted children from Russia. All of our histories had been written in the records together, just waiting for me to open up and read.

Deep connections already exist, and more are coming to us based on the records that we are writing right now. Living in the moment of soul choice and higher intention opens our records to every powerful connection and creates the ultimate Akashic Cause.

The Akashic Cause

The message is clear. Connecting with the Akashic Field is a game-changer. Dynamic vibrations of pure potential can be consciously tapped – or they can even just magically come your way. You have the power to make this a real force in your life. By lifting your own life force with the balanced intentions of self-honoring, action, and loving compassion, your resonant vibration can synchronize with the flow of Universal power, making your goals a record reality.

But it's not just about wanting something. There are plenty of people who want to win the lottery, and they take action every week. Yet only the tiniest percentage of players connect with the winning numbers. And while it's fine to want wealth – and to be wealthy – the Akashic Records reveal with absolute certainty that we are already wealthy beyond measure.

The greatest Akashic Cause is to live in the heart of purpose and appreciation, to be ever conscious of your soul's intentions and ever grateful for each precious moment that is your life's expression. The work that you do, the healing you seek, the peace and joy that you long for – engaging in all of this with courage and perseverance is a causal choice that resonates with life itself. And the Akashic Effect is a life full of profound connections and miraculous occurrences just waiting to come your way!

SUMMARY

♦ Entrainment – or matching resonance – is a type of energetic synchronicity that can bring about amazing and often unexpected consequences.

♦ Unlimited information and boundless creativity fill every corner of the cosmos and can be triggered by the alignment of your intention and action.

♦ Revelations from the records can be spontaneously inspired or purposefully sought, and sometimes the information imposes itself (perhaps with the help of spirit) through an unplanned occurrence that may seem like an accident.

♦ Synchronicity generates its own special magic and your records are a part of an incredible tapestry of boundless information and vibrating cause and effect.

♦ Your higher self is a hologram that has your truth written deep within, and its wonderful vibrations and powerful qualities can be accessed any time you need them.

Part IV
THE RECORDS NEVER END

*'Dreams are illustrations for the
book your soul is writing.'*
MARSHA NORMAN

Chapter 10

Future Records:
The Time Is Now

We have seen how the records can reveal information about the past, and help to shift the present, but they are not limited to that. The Akashic Records exist in all space and all time, and they can offer important insights about your potential future. Remember, however, that the future always vibrates in energetic *potential.* The records are not written in stone; they are determined by our own present (and past) energy – and by the resonance of all those involved.

If you recall the incredible story from Chapter 3 (*see page 46*) about the book that virtually predicted the sinking of the *Titanic,* you might think that some events are absolutely predestined. Yet it's clear that the intentions and choices of the people involved could have changed that outcome in significant ways. The same is true for you – and for the future of your family, your country, and the planet itself.

The Akashic Records hold the visions of *all* the future potentials that could come your way, including the ones that are most likely to happen based on your present energies and actions. As such, viewing those future potentials could be an invaluable tool to assist you in making your ongoing present choices.

The key word here is *potential*.

You have the power to mold your future outcomes according to your own desires and higher intentions, backing them up with your present energies. It's not just about plans or preparation, not just wishful thinking or idle hoping. It's much more energetic – and Akashic – than that!

Fast forward

A client named Virginia was interested in looking at the future potentials regarding her career. She did the 'Viewing future potential' exercise (see page 194) in order to check out her likelihood of getting a promotion based on her present energy and circumstances.

In her opening intention, she requested 'To see her potential career future based on what was going on in the present.' You can imagine her surprise when she opened the video records and saw a future scene playing out where she was getting a divorce!

In the vision, she was seated across from her husband at a large table with lawyers on each side. They were arguing about the custody of the kids, and her husband said, 'Why should you want joint custody? You haven't been a mother to these kids since you got that promotion – and you haven't been a wife to me since you started going after it!'

Virginia had asked to see the future, and she certainly got a glimpse of what was to come. What was more important, though, was that the records were giving her a strong and clear message about the present, and that message woke her up.

She hadn't realized that she had become obsessed with getting this promotion – so much so, she had let go of a lot of her activities with her two kids, missing soccer games and piano recitals, and often coming home from work long after the kids had gone to bed. Her husband picked up the slack and tried to be flexible, but her absence had become so extreme, he even started to wonder if she were having an affair.

The outcome she saw in the records answered the question about work and clearly indicated that she got the promotion. But it pointed to some difficult and unwanted results as well. Virginia loved her husband and her kids. She didn't want a divorce. In fact, she didn't even want the kind of separation from her family that her recent striving had already caused. She had enjoyed helping the kids with their homework and sitting down to dinner all together, laughing and talking about their days.

She felt very conflicted now, however. Part of her still wanted the promotion – as well as the prestige and money it would bring. Yet she was devastated by the thought that it could lead to a life of loneliness and longing for her beloved family.

She decided to seek the advice of her boss, asking him if it would be possible to still get the promotion and cut back a bit on the evening hours. Although he sympathized with her problem, he told her that it would not be possible to cut back and still be promoted. In fact, he pointed out that once that promotion came through, there would be a lot more travel involved, and she'd be away from her family even more. He wisely told her that she had to decide what was more important to her – and whatever decision she made, she had to learn to be OK with the consequences.

After giving it a lot of thought, Virginia realized that it was not OK to lose the man she loved and the family life they had built together. And she knew she would have to put some effort into re-establishing the closeness they once had. She made a choice to stay in a position that allowed her more time, and she found that she was happier, more relaxed, and enjoying her life more than she had in a long, long time. Although she would have liked the money and the recognition, she understood that it was never going to make her happy if she had to experience it all without the people she loved.

This case shows the inestimable value of looking into potential Future Records. We are empowered when we realize that a future outcome can be changed once we bring our consciousness and clear intention to it. It is, after all, our ongoing choices that determine the direction of our destiny.

As Edgar Cayce indicated, every moment, every choice, every thought is recorded in your personal *Akasha*. Those records feed your future potential whether you are aware of them or not. As you continue to engage consciously in the healthy records of thought, emotion, behavior, action, and spirit that we talked about in Chapter 7, you will bring power and healing to your Present Records and unlimited happiness to your future.

When you think about it, your intentions for the future, whether personal or professional, usually revolve around creating happiness in some way. This is why it can be so helpful to visit the records of the *potential* future – not necessarily to predict outcomes, but to see what you can do to support your intentions in your present choices and actions.

You can use the following exercise to get a glimpse into your Future Records. Remember to pick just one issue at a time. You may find, like Virginia, that the thing you long for most may not turn into the outcome you desire. You may also discover that there are things that you can do now to accelerate your process or make the outcome even happier. Let yourself be open to the guidance you get.

Exercise: Viewing future potential in the Akashic Records

Just as you can use a visit to the Record Library to view the past, you can use the same process to take a look into the records of future potentials – whether it be for yourself, for another, or regarding a more worldly or global concern. You can ask to receive the information in a dream or you can use a meditation to open the records in the way that you feel most comfortable or familiar with. Here are some simple steps that you can use in meditation:

Before you start, pick one particular issue or situation you'd like to get a glimpse of and focus your intention or your question on that. You might phrase it like, 'Show me the results of this job search,' or 'Will I get pregnant and have a healthy baby?' You can also use a less specific intention like, 'Show me my daily life in five years.' This could reveal a lot of information about family, health, career, and other matters.

1. Do a relaxing induction to your meditation. Drop your consciousness into your heart center and let go of any concerns, analysis, or expectations.

2. Sense or see yourself moving to your own Sacred Temple or to the Hall of Records or the Eternal Record Library.

3. Release the need to see (or read) about the exact outcome you desire and open yourself up to any important information you can receive about the situation – and your life.

4. Keeping your focused intention in mind, let yourself open your Personal Record Book or turn to the Record Viewing Screen. It is also helpful to ask for the presence or assistance of your Record guide.

5. See or sense the book opening to just the right page – or see the screen coming to life, ready to give you the information you may need.

6. Calmly view the scenario (or words) you see in response to your question.

7. Take in the information about the future potential you're witnessing with peaceful objectivity. You are being given this information for a reason, so let yourself receive it.

8. If you want to see even further ahead, let yourself move forward in time with the intention to see how that particular situation plays out. Do not ask about other issues, but if you get a variety of information, consider how it may apply to the original issue you focused on.

9. After seeing the event or situation play out, ask your guide if there is anything else you need to know about it. You may also want to ask if there's something in your present life that you can do to direct a healthier, happier outcome.

10. Thank your guide and let yourself come out of the experience gently. Jot down your impressions about both the present and the future regarding this issue.

Letting the future open up

This excursion into the future can seem strange at first, and some people are even afraid to find out what could happen. But this exercise is more instructive than predictive, and it should be viewed in that light. The future is an adventure, a journey that we are setting the stage for in all our present moments. When you use this process, you may need some time to figure out the meaning of the events – or their application to your present situation. Give yourself time, and know that changing the future is always a present option.

There are certain things that you can keep in mind to make it easier, more comfortable, and more productive when you are Future Record gazing:

❖ Remember that the vision you're experiencing is a *potential* future event. Nothing is written in stone. What you are seeing is just one likely outcome based on certain present energy patterns. When Present Records change, Future Records follow suit.

❖ Do *not* be discouraged if the result you're looking for isn't revealed. Instead, investigate any options that can help you to redirect the path that you're on. After you employ the options, you can always visit the future again and see how things may have shifted.

❖ Don't panic if you see something difficult or traumatic happening in the future. Again, you are always free to make changes in your personal, professional, physical, or cognitive patterns. In fact, this is the primary purpose of Future Record reading.

❖ Look lovingly at your future self and as you explore the meaning of the experience, take some time to ask your future identity what he or she would like to tell your present self about your life, your purpose, and the path you're on.

The Akashic Records, your recording studio for the future

Although these two processes may be somewhat similar, there's a big difference between *reading* future potentials and *programming* your desired outcomes in the Record Library.

It's well known that visualizing your goals for the future is an important energetic cause in making your goals a reality. And doing this within the framework of the Future Akashic Records can be a highly effective way of significantly accelerating your intention.

Like all visualizations, you can create mental images of what you want your future to look like and then place those goals or outcomes within your Personal Records. When you're deciding how you want these future images to appear, make sure that you don't limit yourself. Let yourself create images of happiness and personal success that you can get excited about – and that you can believe in. If you tend to see the future with negativity, it will be important to let that go and create valuable new options. The images in your mind – and in the records – need to align with your own energy, consciousness, and expectations.

Here are some things you can do to get ready to program Future Akashic Records for yourself:

1. Create successful and happy images of yourself

What is the picture of how you want yourself to be, feel, act, and look like? No matter how distant this ideal self of yours may feel, let yourself create the image in your mind. Meditate on it and feel its energies. Believe in the possibility of this successful and happy image of yourself and take some time each day to view this happy self of yours moving through this daily life. Use the process to program this wonderful self-image in your records often.

2. Create successful joyous images of the outcomes of your goals

Make sure you view your desired record results exactly as you want them to be. Put yourself in the center of the image and allow yourself to feel the joy and excitement of the finished achievement. Sometimes it's helpful to write a narrative of the successful completion of the goal. Then you can visualize yourself putting this written passage into your Future Record Book.

You may have to be flexible in your images of your goals as you work toward these end results. Be open to options, yet always devoted to the optimistic view of your own happy future. As your future evolves, you can get more detailed about the experience to come, filling in facts about your environment, your home, work, and even vacations. Think big and record bigger!

Visualization is a powerful technique, and adding the emotional elements of happiness and excitement enhances that power significantly. Then when you consciously place that joyously charged visual into the records of your future, you can more thoroughly align your specific intentions with the synchronicity of Universal abundance and flow. And when your Personal Records weave harmoniously with the Records of the Universe, real magic happens!

Exercise: Future-Record programming

There are many ways that you can plant the seeds of future achievement into your Personal Records files. An easy, shorter version is described below, but in a more formal version, you could utilize the steps described in the previous exercise, 'Viewing future potential' (see page 194), yet with a different intention. Instead of asking to see a potential outcome related to a specific situation, simply open the viewing screen and allow yourself comfortably to witness the desired end results that you have already mapped out in your visualization. Let yourself witness the exciting achievement of your goal, and then direct your Personal Records to receive this as your truth.

Although a guide isn't necessary in this version of Future Record creating, you can ask your guide to be with you (see page 151). Also, upon completion of viewing your intended recording, you can ask your guide if they have any advice that can help you make this dream come true. When you are finished with this experience, give the successful images to your record guide and to the expansive vibrations of the records themselves, trusting that you have recorded your intention in a very powerful place.

The following version utilizes your Sacred Temple or Record Library (see page 52), and you can bring your guide or record angels into this experience as well. These are all powerful elements that can be helpful as they become more and more familiar to you. This, however, is a shorter and simpler process of future-record programming. It's something that can be done just a few minutes each day, yet it can have very powerful results. In fact, the more often you do this exercise, the more fun it will become. You will feel the presence of the helpful spirits, and you will deeply sense their support.

Here are the steps to the simple process of Future-Record programming:

1. Have the details, images, and emotions of your visualization already planned out in your mind. Use only one goal per programming session. It's sometimes helpful to write a narrative of the outcome ahead of time, describing the details and the emotions that go along with it.

2. The best time for doing this easy exercise is right before falling asleep, when you are tired and your brain frequency is already tending to drift into alpha level. Make sure you have no distractions like the television on in the background. However, you might like to have some gentle music playing.

3. Breathe deeply and let yourself relax. As you do, gently let your consciousness float to your Sacred Temple or Record Library, where you meet your guide or record angel.

4. Continue to relax, and let yourself happily watch the wonderful images of your successful outcomes play out on your Record Screen or come to life in your Future Record Book. See them play out, as you desire them to go, and feel the joy that the images bring.

5. As the image starts to wrap up, affirm that you are placing this experience into the records of your future reality. Then visualize your guide or angels lifting the image into the energetic realm, the realm of all possibilities. As they do, thank them and know that they will be working on your goal as well.

Do this simple process for at least a few days – or perhaps a few weeks. Do not obsess about it, just release it into the Realm of Records and let all concerns go.

Support your Future Record intention with your daily energy of action and self-honoring. As you go through your day, consciously release any thoughts that promote self-doubt or disbelief. If the image comes to mind, give it to the loving Record Spirits who will continue to add their assistance to your own energetic endeavors. Always choose to hold a happy view of yourself and your future life no matter what the details might look like.

Planting the records in future time

A friend of mine had been wanting a bigger house since his second child was born. He had a vision of what it would look like in his mind, and every night for just a few minutes he would visualize his family living in it, and then he would place the image in his Future Records. Finally, he would just let it go, adopting an attitude of peace and trust.

After a few months of this, he was poring over the real estate section of the paper and he saw the very house he had been imagining. Unfortunately, he found out it cost more than he had set aside. He didn't know how he was going to make up the difference for the down payment required, so he decided to use the same technique to get the extra money. Part of him was worried the house would be sold, but he refused to get urgent about it, telling himself that he could always find another.

He did the visualization – this time seeing himself receiving a check for the amount he needed. He continued this process of Future Record writing for several weeks, and he sometimes wondered if it was going to pay off. Whenever his doubts came up, however, he would release the feeling of need, giving the image to the angels or just placing it in his Future Record Book.

It took some time, but he actually did receive a check for the amount he needed – plus some! It turned out that a little property that he and his brothers had inherited had finally sold after years on the market, and his share covered the difference he was looking for, plus a little extra. Of course, he was thrilled that the house he had found months earlier was still available. He was able to purchase it, and the visions that he inscribed in his Future Records became his reality.

This may seem unlikely, but it *is* more than possible to record the reality that you desire. Let yourself see the image and place it in your records, then let it go. If there is action you need to take, do so with a peaceful heart and mind. Make sure you support your intention for future happiness by choosing to enjoy every bit of happiness and peace that you can right now. Know you are inscribing those emotions in your Present Records. Remember that your soul is capable of seeing and creating joy in any circumstance. You may not realize it yet, but this is actually your eternal state of being!

Your Soul's Point of View

The soul's view of Earthly life is quite different from our personal view. Consider the soul's perspective as one of an actor taking on a role he or she is going to play. The character's identity is short-lived, but it's very important that the actor creates that character with as many layers as possible. The more layers, the more interesting the character becomes. When that particular production ends, the actor will move on to the next character, bringing with him or her the experiences and insights from the previous role. If the actor's character is suffering in some way, the actor doesn't have to be bothered by it. In fact, the more difficult the character's emotions, the more the actor must prepare, and the greater the depth and range that actor experiences. With every challenging part, the actor learns and grows.

In some ways this is the soul's approach to this present life and repeated lifetimes. The soul knows that our experience on Earth is short, even if we are lucky to live to a very old age. In terms of eternal reality, this current life, no matter how long, is brief. Yet the approach we take within each life is important in terms of our personal and eternal evolution. As time passes, our soul will go on to another life – or role. The soul welcomes the challenges as well as the blessings, for the goals are both joy and personal enlightenment, which are equally important.

The challenges in our life, such as illness, loss, and poverty, are no bigger problems to our eternal self than the character's difficulties are to an actor assuming that character's personality and behavior. All events, whether positive or negative, are crucial opportunities for the soul's evolution. Achieving such goals as self-mastery, growth in wisdom, discipline and expression, the expansion of love, service and compassion are all part of the soul's path to enlightenment.

Your soul writes your records with these purposes in mind. Your eternal self has a greater design for this life experience. At this moment you may not have any conscious awareness of your own higher plan, and you may be looking at your obstacles with frustration. Such ordeals as mental or emotional attachments, ego and self-esteem issues, longing, loneliness, or poverty can certainly get in the way of your happiness and success, but learning how to heal and transcend them is a part of your ongoing process.

Big changes will begin when you start to look at things from your Soul's Point of View.

*Know that in every experience is a lesson that
will help you realize this important truth: What
you learn is more valuable than the event itself.*

In fact, it's not what happens to you, but how you react to what happens to you that really matters. You have the power to see your eternal truth, to call upon your Akashic Forces and bring courage, peace, and Divine wisdom into any present moment. When you connect with the lesson at hand, you can live with the equanimity that your Akashic perspective brings, moving your life forward with purpose and understanding. This is the ultimate Akashic Truth: Your soul is the solution. Free yourself of conflict and live in the peace of non-striving, the beautiful peace of the soul.

SUMMARY

◆ Future events exist in energetic potential, and you can visit them to determine what you would like to change now in order to create the most desirable outcomes later.

◆ You can use your Akashic Records Screen as a recording studio of the future for energized attraction and manifestation.

◆ By creating positive images of yourself and your goals, you can secure those pictures in your Future Records.

◆ As difficult as any situation is, your soul knows that every event brings a valuable opportunity to learn, heal, and grow.

Chapter 11

Akashic Purpose, Power, and Inspiration

A *Christmas Carol* by Charles Dickens hasn't been out of print since its first publication in 1843. It has been translated into dozens of languages and converted into countless plays, TV shows, and theatrical productions. This is the story of a miserly old man who changes his life – and the lives of many others – through a personal epiphany. But did you know that this tenderhearted and moving story is about the Akashic Records?

Think about it for a moment. This elderly gentleman (through the help of spirit) is able to go back and witness his choices and circumstances of the past. He is also able to investigate the present and witness the options and adjacent possibilities that his present moments hold. Finally, he is taken into the records of his potential future – a future that seems inevitable based on his present behavior, attitude, and choices – a future where both he and the sweet child Tiny Tim pass away by Christmas of the following year.

He realizes through these various travels through time and experiences in the records that he no longer wants to pursue the same path that he is on. In fact, when looking upon his own headstone, Scrooge is driven to pleading with the Ghost of Christmas Yet to Come. He says:

Men's courses will foreshadow certain ends, to which, if persevered in, they must lead... But if the courses be departed from, the ends will change. Good Spirit... Assure me that I yet may change these shadows you have shown me by an altered life.

The ghost doesn't respond to him, but Scrooge learns his answer upon waking up on Christmas morning. When he realizes he is still alive, his spirit is renewed and filled with deep appreciation and excitement for life. Scrooge then goes on to write wonderful new records in his present life – records filled with compassion, generosity, and a higher purpose of helping his fellow man than he ever had before.

Clearly he viewed and changed his own Future Records, and through Scrooge's loving intervention, Tiny Tim did not die. Scrooge himself lived on and became known for his exuberance. It was said of him that he knew how to keep Christmas well, and that he kept it in his heart throughout the year, a function of writing joyous Present Records.

Though Dickens never identified it, Scrooge was a man who used the incredible power of the Akashic Records, the information brought by spirit and held in the ethers, to his benefit and to the benefit of many others. Marley's ghost had interceded for Scrooge and predicted his reclamation, revealing another important function of the Akashic Records: ***Foretelling the possible future and viewing present options in order to create change there.***

At first look, *A Christmas Carol* is just a sweet, cautionary tale reminding us not to live in misery and constant striving. Above that, of course, is the moral reminder that we should prioritize our social responsibility and our understanding that we are all indeed connected. But on a higher level, it tells us that we are capable of looking into the past and the future, and if we are open to the information there – in the Akashic Records – we can shift the quality of our life at its core.

Inspiration from the Akashic Records

A Christmas Carol is not only a story *about* the Akashic Records, it is also an example of how the Akashic Records can reach into the mind of man and inspire greatly. In fact, it is my belief that this story – so beautifully penned – was actually inspired and given to Dickens by the records themselves. In a letter to a friend, Dickens described how he received the opening scene of the book in a dream, which is not an uncommon way to receive Akashic Record information. Dickens was also in the habit of walking through the streets of London late at night, thinking about the work he was currently writing.

These were walking meditations of sorts, where his mind would wander and be filled with ideas of where to take his story next. He told one friend that his walks during the writing of *A Christmas Carol*, which were sometimes more than 10 miles a night, were filled with images and ideas.

After some sleep, he would write those ideas down, and then later that evening go out and receive more inspiration to be woven into the plot, characters, and dialogue. He didn't realize it, of course, but he was connecting with the inspiration of the Akashic Records, giving to the world a truly enduring and important piece of work, entertaining, compelling, and inspiring people for over 170 years.

My belief that Dickens was connected to the Akashic Records in the production of this story is by no means meant to disparage his ability as a writer. In fact, it's just the opposite. As we saw in Chapter 9, it's the people that have the greatest ability that are often inspired the most. Their energy, intention, and action resonate so strongly with the Akashic Realm that an open, flowing pipeline is created and the Universe is blessed by the results.

Whatever you would like to be inspired about, the Akashic Field is always open to you. Albert Einstein received his inspiration for the theory of relativity while riding on a bus. In fact, many people tap into the creative information they need either while dreaming or daydreaming. Meditation and relaxation can be a source of solution as well.

All you have to do is to create a focused intention – or even just be willing to receive inspiration and discovery of any kind. Weave that intention into your daily life, then relax and let go. You can also ask for assistance from the spirits and guides we talked about earlier. The Universe wants to promote expression, creativity, evolution, and enlightenment. Your determination to grow and bring some sort of betterment to the world aligns with Universal intention and will touch your heart and mind.

Exercise: Invoking record assistance

Whatever guidance or inspiration you seek, whether it's about a work project, a scientific endeavor, a piece of creative expression, or a resolution to some personal or professional problem, you can receive dramatic guidance. The following little invocations will help to open those record doors for you. Say any of these – or use your own – before you fall asleep or before meditating, and then let yourself open up to receiving.

'I invite the presence of the loving Record Spirits, and I am grateful for all of the helpful, healing information I receive.'

'I am connecting with the energy and guidance of the great Akashic Field. The Records are open to me now and I am open to receiving all the information I seek.'

'My heart and mind are always open to the wisdom and direction of the Akashic Realm. I receive inspiration in wonderful and unexpected ways.'

This simple request or intention of connection opens you up to receiving important information from the Akashic Records. I myself experienced this with rather significant results, as the following case study illustrates.

The Akashic Records respond

I had been working with a client who was having serious difficulty being confident at work. Peggy had had self-esteem issues her whole life, and we worked on making her more comfortable in social situations, with her family, and even in romantic relationships. It took some time but she slowly became more and more comfortable in her own skin. The one place where she still had quite a bit of anxiety, however, was at work. She was stuck in a job that she didn't like, and she fully believed that she was not capable or smart enough to go any further.

We had used affirmations and meditation to help her in the other areas, and in time she was able to break through. But she was so hard on herself in the professional arena, it seemed she simply could not get comfortable or confident in any situation there.

I was thinking about Peggy's situation as I was going to bed one night, wishing that I could help her see the beautiful truth within her – and help her relax in her work environment. As I was falling asleep, I said right out loud, 'There must be something easy that Peggy could do to change all this.'

It was a simple statement, but it felt more like a request – or even like a directive to the Universe, a supplication for help.

That night I had a dream that revealed an incredibly simple technique that when used with affirmative statements can completely shift your energy and your experience. It incorporated a very easy position, placing your fingertips at your brow chakra, which is also called the third eye or the energy center between your eyebrows. The dream explained to me in detail exactly how the position should look, and it gave me specific statements for decoding negative patterns and coding healthy and beneficial truths instead. It *was a beautifully easy, yet elegant technique that actually accelerates and energizes your intention for radical results.*

I taught Peggy this special position, and she became more and more comfortable, assertive, and expressive in work. Now she is an executive in an international company running huge conferences where before she could hardly run a sales meeting of 10 or 12 people.

Later, I wrote a book called Your Quantum Breakthrough Code, *describing how to use the process in exactly the same way I had been told in that dream. Now I receive emails from people all over the world telling me how the Quantum Breakthrough Code has changed their lives, healing phobias, addictions, unhappiness, and more. But I'm the first to say that it didn't come from me. I needed a certain solution, genuinely wanted to help Peggy, expressed my intention, and the great Akashic Field of wisdom and information rose to my mind, bringing the information I was seeking.*

> *Any statement, any invocation, any heartfelt request can open the record doors for you – even when you least expect it.*

So let yourself voice your intention – and then let it go. Whether you're hoping to help another, work on a professional project, learn a new skill, or enhance a personal talent, the assistance you seek is waiting to open up for you in the Akashic Realm.

Building your talent team

Akashic inspiration can come in the areas of your personal skills and talents, lifting your abilities to new heights. In fact, there is much to learn and be inspired by in the Akashic Records, and there are wonderful spirits who can help to bring that information to you – especially in the areas of personal interests and talents.

These may be past-life acquaintances of yours, or legends and masters who engaged in similar endeavors in history. They could also be members of ancient societies, bringing inspiration from an era that resides deep in your eternal memory, embedded in the *Akasha* of all time. Even if you're not quite sure what talent or practice you want to pursue, the answers can be found in the records as well.

Also, if you feel you've had a past life that embraced the talent that you are interested in today, you can use the past-life viewing technique described in Chapter 6 (*see page 104*) to call upon that experience. Create a focused intention referring to the talent or skill you desire to develop, one that takes you back to a life where you were successful at this particular activity. You may see yourself using techniques that you are presently unaware of. You may also meet teachers and scholars from that life that now reside in the spiritual plane and are willing to guide you in your present pursuits. Once you know these wonderful beings, you can use the exercise below to continue to call on them for their help and inspiration.

But your talent team isn't limited to people you've been with in past lives. It could include some of the greatest masters of the ages, the legends in their field. If you're in politics, your spirit guide could be a great leader in history. If science or invention is your pursuit, don't be surprised if Einstein or Edison answers your call. If art, music, or journalism speaks to you, you can turn to such entities as Degas, Chopin, or Edward R. Murrow.

You see, these great thinkers loved their fields of study and expression, and they long to continue and to help you as well. So don't think someone is too famous to know who you are or to want to help you in your search for excellence. Their presence may surprise you, but don't let your doubt stop you.

Artistic connection

I was once doing a reading for a client who was an artist. She painted in oils and watercolors and achieved some success. She wanted to take her art to the next level, however, and she didn't quite know how. In our reading I saw a man standing behind her at the easel, whispering in her ear. When I asked who this man was, I heard the name Monet.

But she had loved Monet and regarded him so highly that she was hesitant to believe me. She asked why someone so great would want to help her, who had some local fame but hadn't broken through to the national level. I said that fame didn't matter; there must be a resonance that drew him to her. As we talked, that resonance became clear. Monet was her favorite artist. In fact, she had gone to study and paint in Giverny in France, where Monet had spent much of his artistic life.

Seeing the connection, she finally accepted that he could be there for her, and she called upon him regularly. She received ideas in dreams and while working at her easel. In fact, she told me she could sometimes feel him there. In time, her art – and her fame – started to soar!

You can use the following exercise to call on specific talent spirits or to invite the help of any helpful guide to assist you in your life. Your present interests precede this life, so you can call upon a past-life guide as well. In fact, you can build an entire talent team, a dream team of guides that can help you with any project or concern. And if you prefer, you can use the screen of your Sacred Temple (*see page 52*) to see yourself engaging in the activity.

Exercise: Inspiration from the legends of the ages

Think of all the legends through the ages that have inspired you – the great scientists, artists, poets, philosophers, politicians, and leaders. Many people in ancient and recent times have sent their energy to your heart, your mind, and your life. You can either call someone by name, or you can think of the pursuit you'd like to receive information about and be open to whomever comes to you. Don't think that people are too famous or too important to respond to you. When they were in the physical world, they sought to bring their vision to the world, and now they wish to do the same for you. These spirits enjoy lending their influence to your life, your purposes, and your dreams.

1. Let yourself relax. Breathe deeply and let your muscles go loose, limp, and relaxed.

2. Take another deep breath and let your consciousness drift gently into your heart center. Let all of the muscles in your body continue to relax.

3. Relax even further and let your mind and your consciousness float to your own beautiful Sacred Temple.

4. Go in and sit down in your big, comfortable chair. As you do, let yourself think about the spirit expert you'd like to call – or a project you'd like guidance with.

5. Remain calm as you begin to feel this person coming to you. Notice if you perceive a name, an energy, or colors. Feel this person's energy peacefully moving through and around you.

6. Ask this guide about a situation in your life or profession. It could be a current project, a skill, or it could be something about which you have yet to learn. Let this person give you some information about it now.

7. Let yourself receive the information in a way that's comfortable to you. It may come in the form of a word, a phrase, or an image.

8. Now let this guide show you any actions he or she would take. Be open to receiving any guidance or techniques.

9. Feel this person's talents gently moving through you, through your hands, your mind, your heart, your voice. You feel filled with profound talent and creative forces.

10. Now take a moment to think about the project you have in mind. See it in a completed state with beautiful light all around it. You feel a passion and excitement, which grows as you notice your guide pouring light and energy into your project, too.

11. Thank your talent guide now, knowing that you have created a strong bond here today. You know that you can turn to this guide – and many others – whenever you need ideas, inspiration, or direction.

12. Let yourself come back to this time and space now, remembering everything you experienced here.

In the days, weeks, and months to come you will receive more and more inspiration. You will receive it in dreams, in messages, and in flashes of intuition. Let yourself trust the information you get. Know that you can ask for help and guidance from your talent guides any time that you desire.

Open your mind and heart to meeting the wonderful, legendary teachers and masters of the ages. Don't be shy or think you're unworthy. You are a unique voice in the world, and the legends of the ages want to help you be heard. In fact, it may be a part of your soul's purpose to find your talent and – with the help of the Record Spirits – to share it.

The pursuit of purpose

At their core, your Akashic Records are a map of your soul's path through eternity. Your soul has a purpose for coming to this Earthly experience. In fact, there could be a number of purposes your deeper intentions are guiding you to, including spiritual and personal purposes – and your purpose in the world.

Your spiritual purpose might lean to such pursuits as connecting with spirit, releasing inner conflict and finding a greater peace within – or surrendering attachment and finding a purer form of happiness. Such endeavors can be closely related to your personal purpose as well, for your psychology is closely linked to your spirituality.

Your personal purpose is more about the experiences of your daily life – but these cannot, and should not, be separated from your soul's intention to achieve a deeper level of spirituality. Yet personally, your soul's directives may be telling you to let go of patterns of fear and worry, or to raise your courage and speak your truth, or to learn how to be more loving toward yourself or others.

Understanding and navigating your relationships is often a part of your personal purpose. Whether they are romantic, platonic, family, or even professional relationships, they can hold many challenges. You may need to learn how to honor yourself and hold your own, or how to communicate your needs, or even how to let go. Whatever your personal purpose may be, you can probably take a look at your life, and if you're honest with yourself, be able to see what your soul wants you to do.

Some people think that having a purpose in the world means the action has to be taken on a worldwide – or at least broad – scope. But your purpose in the world can be far-reaching in a more personal way. Being a loving and supportive parent can be one of the greatest purposes in the world – and the effects of your choices in that pursuit can reach forward in time for generations to come. Your world purpose may also be found in your professional and creative endeavors, the action of which reaches out as well.

It's easy to see how all of these pursuits overlap. For example, if you learn to love and value yourself more, you can be happier and more peaceful in your family and personal life – and more creative and productive in your work in the world. Your soul knows that as you follow your Akashic Path, which is the larger directive of your soul, you will be on the road to arriving at all of these destinations.

Some people don't know what their purpose in this life is, and they often feel lost and at sea, wondering what they should do next. You can use the records to find this out for yourself. And even if you know what your soul's directives are, it's often enlightening to look at your Book of Purpose to get more clarity.

Use the following technique to gain access to this information – and to receive guidance about how your purpose can be achieved. You can return to this technique whenever you need clarity about a specific goal, relationship or personal pursuit.

Exercise: Your Book of Purpose

The following exercise is a process that takes you to your Book of Purpose in your Hall of Records. You may ask what is your spiritual, personal, or relationship purpose. Or you could just open it up and read the insights there. Invite your soul to direct you and then simply follow the steps of the process and open up to receiving guidance on what your purpose is and what steps you can take to move toward that.

1. Take a deep breath and relax. Let your consciousness drift gently down into your heart center.

2. Continue to relax as you feel the peace of your heart center filling you up. You begin to notice a stately building in front of you, with a sign that says, 'Your Hall of Records.'

3. Let yourself enter the building and look around you. You notice in the center of the room is a tall wooden table or podium with a beautiful large book on it.

4. You look at the book and you see your name on the cover with the words, 'Your Book of Purpose.' You know that the wisdom and power of your eternal self brings information through this source, including any guidance you seek about your purpose – or anything else.

5. Remaining peaceful and relaxed, you can now state your intention or ask a question about your purpose. You slowly start to notice the book in front of you open up, flipping to just the right page to give you the guidance that you seek.

6. You notice the book settles on a certain page. The page may have words written on it or an image floating above it. Let yourself see or sense whatever feels natural to you. Either way, this presents some information to reveal your purpose and to let you see how you can make it come about. Just take a moment to get some details now. You may only get it in bits and pieces, but rest assured the information will fill in over time.

7. You start to feel a sensation of understanding and receptivity as the seed of purpose touches your heart.

8. And now you start to notice the pages of the book flipping again, falling open to give you more insight.

9. Just let yourself receive and accept. You may intuitively know what this means but you will also receive deeper understanding about this as time goes on.

10. And now you can let it all go. You know you can come to the Hall of Records any time. All the guidance you need is waiting for you here.

Making Akashic choices

Following your purpose will lead you to many situations where you'll be faced with different choices, clearly leading to potentially different outcomes. Whenever you're looking at different options and find that you have a choice to make, you can search the Akashic Records to find the answers you need.

We have to make countless decisions throughout our lives. Some come in routine, day-to-day, moments, like what to have for dinner or what to wear to work. Most of these types of choices can be made according to our intuition or preference at the time. There are other seemingly routine choices that would best be made by simply asking, 'Which choice honors me the most?'

In fact, this question is the first line of reasoning in making any decision. Whatever you're doing – or choosing – ask yourself, 'Does this honor me?' This approach will keep you moving forward on your soul's path. The intention to honor yourself recognizes your eternal worth. It also helps you to make more healthy and beneficial decisions and keeps you on the path of self-mastery.

It's never dishonoring to another if you choose to honor yourself. Of course, others may get frustrated and even angry if you start to move in this direction after having accepted dishonoring in the past. But if this is the case, the choice to self-honor is definitely one of your soul's purposes. So use this as your inner barometer. If you are honest with yourself, you will know in your heart what honors you. And when you do, you may need to muster up some courage and strength in order to make the honoring choice.

Once you've determined what honors you, there will still be decisions that you need to make. For example, deciding which college to go to, which city to relocate to, which job to take, or even what stock to pick – all of these could very well be life-changing decisions. And the Akashic Records hold information about the potential outcomes of each choice.

There are two processes you can use to investigate your options when you have to make a decision. Both reveal information from the records, but in vastly different ways. The first is a process called billet reading. The second involves looking at your soul's map.

The word *billet* comes from the French meaning 'ticket.' The process of reading billets is fairly easy, but – like all of the processes in this book – it requires the ability to trust your intuition. The billet process is used when you have multiple options and want to discern which one is best.

Exercise: Reading billets for multiple choices

Before following this process, consider the specific issue you want information about. For example, if you're looking at three different universities, consider the logistical reasons for your choices first. If you're still unsure, go on to the exercise below.

1. Simply write the name or data about each option on small pieces of paper (hence the word billet). Put each piece of paper into an envelope then seal it. All the envelopes must be the same shape and color so as not to single any one option out.

2. Lay out the individual envelopes separately on a table in front of you. Take a deep breath and clear your mind. Relax and release any concern about the issue.

3. Pick up one envelope and hold it in your hands. (Some people prefer to hold it near the heart or heart center.) Take a moment to notice any sensations or feelings that come to you. You may feel a lifting of your spirit, or a sense of dread, or even a feeling of fatigue. Then spend a few moments writing down your feelings on the envelope itself.

4. Also let yourself notice if any words, phrases, or images come to mind and jot those down on the envelope as well. When you've written all your impressions on that particular envelope, set it aside.

5. Once you put that billet down, take a few cleansing deep breaths. Clear your mind and let go of all the previous thoughts and sensations. It may be helpful to stretch out or have a sip of water before you go on.

6. When you feel clear, pick up the next envelope and follow the same procedure. Continue doing this until you have finished with all of the envelopes on the table.

When you're done with all the envelopes, you can then open them to identify each option and read the Akashic Impressions you have written about each one. Most will reveal rather obvious messages. For example, one envelope may read, 'tired, worried, running late, alone.' This could indicate that the university named inside may be stressful, packed with work and short on friends. However, if another billet reads, 'sun, bird, moving fast,' it could indicate happier times, feelings of freedom, and time going quickly.

These are clear answers, but some of your impressions may be more vague, and may not give you as clear direction as you desire. If this is the case, you can use the soul map exercise opposite or the 'Viewing future potential' exercise in Chapter 10 (see page 194).

Exercise: Your soul's map

You can either use the Sacred Temple approach to view your maps on the screen, or you can use your Hall of Records and open the map in your Record Book. Have your Record Journal with you to write down your impressions.

1. Let yourself relax and pick one of the above viewing approaches, as you think about the question you have in mind.

2. As you relax even further, you see a map in front of you. (It may even appear as a screen on a GPS.)

3. State your question, such as: 'Show me the road ahead if I should follow this path (make this decision, go to this school, etc.).'

4. Slowly you see the map come to life and a light on the road starts moving forward.

5. You follow the light and notice street signs that you're passing. They aren't the names of streets, though. Instead, they are descriptive words, some of which evoke feelings in you.

6. The street signs may read, for example, 'fun,' 'romance,' 'hard work,' or even 'keep on going,' or 'turn back now.' You may even see images like flowers, birds, or buildings. Just remain calm and relaxed and take note of the places the road is taking you.

7. In time the street signs will fade and you will know you're at the end of this particular journey.

8. When you're finished, take some time to jot down your impression in your Record Journal. Even if you didn't get much information – or if it was unclear to you – you will begin to have a deeper understanding as time goes on.

Remember that the future exists in pure potential, and the answers you receive indicate potential outcomes, consequences that are based on present energy patterns. As you change your energy – and as the energy of the situation changes – you could find different results awaiting you.

Also remember that your soul has designs and purposes you may not be aware of yet. I used this exercise when considering my choice to marry my second husband. I had a difficult marriage and divorce the first time around, and I really wanted to get it right. So I opened my map and followed the road that marriage would take me down. I saw words like 'enlightenment,' 'new beginnings,' and 'world travel.'

All of this was quite exciting to me, and I felt it was destined to be a great experience. But I found out over time that we had significant differences that couldn't be ignored. We resonated intellectually, but we just couldn't make the rest of the marriage work.

So I wondered about what seemed to be a mistaken message on that map. As time went on, however, I came to realize what it meant. Although the marriage ended, it had provided me with a truly life-changing experience. It was my second husband who introduced me to quantum physics and to the principles and theories that formed the concepts that I write about in my books and teach in seminars all over the world. If I hadn't married him, it's highly unlikely that I would have ever become aware of the energetic principles that are now the backbone of my personal and professional life. In some ways, that failed marriage opened up the Akashic Records for me!

However you do it, looking into the future can be interesting and fun. But it shouldn't be taken lightly. Reading billets isn't just a parlor trick. You're not just pulling the right answers out of a hat. In both of these processes you are calmly sending your consciousness into the Akashic Field to get information to enhance your life and to reveal your soul's intention.

This requires trust and tranquility. It requires letting go of desperation and attachment to outcome. The Akashic Records are always available, not only to direct you, but to charge your life with purpose, wisdom and fulfillment, vital energies that raise your vibration and bring you far greater synchronicity with the Universe you live in. When you resonate with authenticity and genuine awareness of your power and value in the world, you will find magic and mystery unfolding before you. You will be living an Akashic Life.

SUMMARY

+ You can create focused intentions for personal or professional purposes and weave them into your daily life. Continue to take action, then relax and let go.

+ Build your talent team by calling on specific spirit guides or asking for help with a specific purpose. Open your heart and trust what you receive.

+ Your soul has a purpose for coming to this Earthly experience, and the Akashic Records are a map of your soul's path through eternity.

♦ Whenever you're looking at different options and find that you have a choice to make, you can search the Akashic Records to find the answers you need.

♦ Looking into your Future Records is a powerful way of getting information to enhance your life and reveal your soul's intention.

Conclusion:
The Akashic Life

Your soul's path has brought you to this very moment in time. Everything in the long expanse of your eternal life has led you here. This moment is a turning point. What do you want to do now?

There are things for you to learn, do, and achieve here in this life, and the records of your soul's truth can show you the way. When you continue to connect with this truth, you open the pipeline to ancient wisdom and future discovery, to inner peace and outer achievement.

Let go of mental striving and live in your heart. This heart-centered resonance is one of the most profound links to the vast and vibrating Akashic Realm. So breathe deeply and let yourself live in the power of your soul. The Akashic Forces of wisdom, courage, and freedom are always yours in this identity.

You can lift every moment to a deeper meaning and a more profound experience of your power. Your past and future lives are meeting in the nexus of this very moment. Let yourself feel the energy of boundless love abiding within your own inestimable value right now. Bring the joy and peace of the furthest reaches of heaven into even the tiniest moments of your daily life, your Akashic Life.

You are always free to reinvent
yourself, carve out a new future, and
even rewrite a different past.

Ask yourself one question. If you were to compose your own story, to write the novel where you were the hero (or perhaps the villain?), what would you write about your next scene? What direction would your story go in now? The Akashic Records are the novel of your life, and you are writing the next chapter now, weaving the threads into the tapestry that illustrates the story of your eternal life.

You are the author, the director, and the main character, too. Where you take your records is up to you. Live consciously in as many moments as you can, ever aware of the power in your hands, in your mind, in your vision, and in your choices. And always remember you are always composing your own story in the ever-present now.

So take a step back and look at your life. Try to realize that your soul and its journey are a part of the Akashic Records. Your experiences, your thoughts, your emotions, all of these are a part of the vibrational records that apply to you and to every soul. These records connect and fit together in very specific ways. Your own records forge with others to become a part of the Eternal Records of all time, the vibrational reality that we all share.

This connection to the world is undeniable, and it extends through time and space. Each individual throughout history has their own Personal Energy Field, the vibrations of which join the vibrations of all others, expanding certain energies and intentions in amazing ways. This joint energy connects with the resonance of the environment and with the Universal Consciousness itself, creating a fullness of information and vibration that is, in fact, the source and being of the Akashic Records on an infinite scale.

The most important thing to remember is this:

*There is far more to you – and to your
records – than you could possibly imagine.*

Your Eternal Records hold profound love, Divine thought, the ability to create, and the potential to heal yourself and the world!

And when you connect with this ever-present force, you tap into the power of the Universe itself. Record your present moments and ongoing choices with a higher consciousness of thought and emotion, and you will change the very resonance and quality of your life. Soon your records will show that love, success, happiness and creativity abound in every moment of this, your Akashic Life.

Further Reading

Linda Howe, *Healing Through the Akashic Records* (Sounds True; reprint edition 2016)

Linda Howe, *How to Read the Akashic Records* (Sounds True; reprint edition 2010)

Jess Stearn, Edgar Cayce, *The Sleeping Prophet* (Bantam Doubleday Dell Publishing Group; new edition 1997)

Thomas Sugrue, *There is a River: The Story of Edgar Cayce* (ARE Press; revised edition, 1997)

Sandra Anne Taylor, *The Hidden Power of Your Past Lives* (Hay House, 2014)

Sandra Anne Taylor, *Quantum Success* (Hay House, 2007)

Kevin J. Todeschi, *Edgar Cayce on the Akashic Records* (ARE Press, 1999)

Resources

Books

The following titles are all available from Hay House:

Your Quantum Breakthrough Code: The Simple Technique that Brings Everlasting Joy and Success

Quantum Success: The Astounding Science of Wealth and Happiness

Secrets of Success: The Science and Spirit of Real Prosperity, with Sharon A. Klingler

Secrets of Attraction: The Universal Laws of Love, Sex, and Romance

Truth, Triumph, and Transformation: Sorting Out the Fact from the Fiction in Universal Law

28 Days to a More Magnetic Life

The Hidden Power of Your Past Lives: Revealing Your Encoded Consciousness

The Energy Oracle Cards: 53 Card Deck and Guidebook

Guided visualizations, CDs, and audio programs

Energy Breakthrough Meditations, including:
Power Chakra Clearing, Rescripting Beliefs, Clearing the Road Ahead, and Affirmations for Self-Empowerment

Act to Attract (nine-CD audio seminar and workbook)

Act to Attract Meditations, including: *Attracting Love, Your Sacred Identity,* and *Morning and Evening Affirmations* (CD)

Attracting Success, including: *Attracting Success and Planting Your Destiny Garden,* and *Mystic Journey Music* (CD)

Healing Journeys, including: *Cellular Regression: Timeless Healing* and *Relaxation and Memory Release* (CD)

Contacts

Sandra co-founded (along with Sharon A. Klingler) Starbringer Associates, a speaker and consultant agency that produces events and audio seminars for personal, spiritual, and business enhancement. For more information – or to schedule lectures, seminars, or business or private consultations with Sandra – contact her at:

Sandra Anne Taylor
P.O. Box 362
Avon, OH 44011 USA
www.sandrataylor.net
facebook.com/sandraannetaylor

Or

Starbringer Associates
871 Canterbury Road, Unit B
Westlake, OH 44145 USA
Telephone: +1 440-871-5448
www.starbringerassociates.com

ABOUT THE AUTHOR

Sandra Anne Taylor has been a counselor in a private psychology practice for more than 25 years, working with individuals and couples in the treatment of anxiety, depression, addiction, and relationship issues. Her Quantum Life Coaching Certification program offers powerful techniques for connecting spirit, mind, and manifestation. Her multidimensional approach brings exceptional clarity and practicality to the science of whole-life healing and personal achievement.

She is the *New York Times* best-selling author of several titles including *Quantum Success* and *Your Quantum Breakthrough Code*. Her other titles include *The Hidden Power of Your Past Lives*; *28 Days to a More Magnetic Life*; *Secrets of Attraction*; *Truth, Triumph, and Transformation*; the beautiful – and amazingly accurate – *Energy Oracle Cards*; and *Secrets of Success*, co-authored with Sharon Anne Klingler. Her many popular books are available in 28 languages across the globe.

Sandra is the co-founder of Starbringer Associates, a speaker and consultant agency that produces events and audio seminars for personal, spiritual, and business enhancement (*see page 232 for more information*). Her popular radio show, Living your Quantum Success, can be heard Mondays on HayHouseRadio.com®.

She lives in northern Ohio with her husband and two adopted Russian-born children.

www.sandrataylor.net

Notes

Notes

Notes

Notes